Supporting Students with Dyslexia in Secondary Schools

This is a wonderful book ... well organised, accessible and jargon free. Particularly useful is the link to mainstream subject teaching. Without having to read the whole book, busy teachers and teaching assistants can dip in and out of the text in order to find appropriate strategies. This text should be on the shelf of every secondary school library and cited as suggested reading in training courses.

Dr Lindsay Peer CBE
Chartered Psychologist, Peer Gordon Associates and formerly
Education Director, British Dyslexia Association

This highly practical book focuses on the teaching and learning of students with dyslexia in the context of the mainstream secondary curriculum, and provides practical guidance for school managers and subject teachers by highlighting the barriers to learning experienced by dyslexic learners in today's curriculum.

Full of advice for removing – or minimising – these barriers, this book is packed with strategies for supporting learning and raising the attainment of students with dyslexia. Teachers of students aged 11–19 will find valuable information on:

- how dyslexia affects dyslexic learners' access to and progress in the subject curriculum;
- how secondary teachers can identify possible barriers to learning in their subject delivery;
- the development and provision of appropriate support strategies for meeting the needs of dyslexic students;
- good practice in the identification and assessment of dyslexia that may be masked by high ability or divergent behaviour.

The use of case studies helpfully highlights the impact of dyslexia on students as they transfer to secondary school. They illustrate how and why this condition may be mistaken for behavioural – or other – difficulties, consider whole-school issues and relate throughout the book to a practical framework of proven support strategies.

Moira Thomson was formerly Principal Teacher of Support for Learning at Broughton High School, Edinburgh, and a Development Officer for the City of Edinburgh Department of Children and Families. She is currently an educational consultant, providing Continuing Professional Development for teachers and volunteers in an advisory capacity to local dyslexia organisations and parent groups.

Related Titles from Routledge

Dyslexia: Surviving and Succeeding at College by Sylvia Moody
HB: 978–0–415–43058–6
PB: 978–0–415–43059–3

Teaching Children with Dyslexia: A Practical Guide by Philomena Ott
PB: 978–0–415–32454–0

The Routledge Companion to Dyslexia edited by Gavin Reid,
Gad Elbeheri, Deborah Knight and Janice Wearmouth
HB: 978–0–415–43078–4
PB: 978–0–415–43079–1

Dyslexia at College (3rd edition) by Liz Du Pré, Dorothy Gilroy
and Tim Miles
HB: 978–0–415–40417–4
PB: 978–0–415–40418–1

Supporting Students with Dyslexia in Secondary Schools

Every class teacher's guide to removing barriers and raising attainment

Moira Thomson

Routledge
Taylor & Francis Group

LONDON AND NEW YORK

First published 2008
by Routledge
2 Park Square, Milton Park, Abingdon, Oxon, OX14 4RN

Simultaneously published in the USA and Canada
by Routledge
270 Madison Ave, New York, NY 10016

Routledge is an imprint of the Taylor & Francis Group, an informa business

© 2008 Moira Thomson

Typeset in Sabon
by Florence Production Ltd, Stoodleigh, Devon
Printed and bound in Great Britain
by CPI Antony Rowe, Chippenham, Wiltshire

British Library Cataloguing in Publication Data
A catalogue record for this book is available from the British Library

Library of Congress Cataloging in Publication Data
Thomson, Moira.
   Supporting students with dyslexia in secondary schools/by Moira
   Thomson.
      p. cm.
   Includes bibliographical references.
   1. Dyslexic children—Education (Secondary).   I. Title.
   LC4708.T46 2009
   371.91′44—dc22   2008020283

ISBN10: 0–415–47811–1 (pbk)
ISBN10: 0–203–88809–X (ebk)

ISBN13: 978–0–415–47811–3 (pbk)
ISBN13: 978–0–203–88809–4 (ebk)

To the late Linda Christie, friend and colleague, who persuaded me to stop talking and start writing

Contents

Acknowledgements

My thanks to:

Dyslexia Scotland for permission to include material from their publication: Thomson, M. (2007) *Supporting Dyslexic Pupils in the Secondary Curriculum*, which was issued free to all secondary schools in Scotland.

Paul Chapman Publishing for permission to include photocopiable material from their publication: Thomson, M. (2006) *Supporting Gifted & Talented Pupils in the Secondary School*.

Dr Margaret Crombie and Hilary McColl for their permission to include Table 6.1, which we produced together for presentation at the BDA International Conference at Warwick University in March 2004.

Meg Houston and David Dodds for not complaining when I picked up and developed topics we discussed together.

Alasdair Andrew, Karen Reid and the committee of Dyslexia Scotland South East for supporting this work in every way.

Alison and Lucy of Routledge and Jude Bowen of Sage for their support.

The dyslexic people I have worked with, who taught me all I know.

CHAPTER 1

Identification of dyslexia in secondary schools

In this chapter, readers will:

- become aware of some of the issues surrounding dyslexia;

- look at the three main areas of research into the causes of dyslexia;

- consider current definitions of dyslexia;

- examine the characteristics of dyslexia that might be observed in the classroom;

- look at case studies to set dyslexia in context;

- develop awareness that multilingualism and co-morbid conditions may delay the identification of dyslexia;

- understand that students sometimes deliberately conceal their difficulties;

- learn to recognise patterns of behaviour that might indicate the presence of dyslexia in students.

Background

For many years dyslexia has been surrounded by controversy, largely due to differing views of 'experts' about the nature of this disability. The term 'dyslexia' comes from the Greek and means 'difficulty with words' but over the years, dyslexia has become the term commonly used to refer to a condition, probably neurobiological in origin (British Dyslexia Association (BDA) 2007) that affects reading, spelling, writing, memory, concentration, personal organisation and self-esteem.

It is generally accepted that dyslexia tends to run in families and continues throughout life and that, although dyslexic people can develop strategies for dealing with their difficulties, these never actually go away. Dyslexia occurs in people from all backgrounds and of all abilities and varies in degree from those who cannot read at all to those who achieve university degrees (Dyslexia Action 2005).

In the 1970s and 1980s there was considerable debate about whether dyslexia actually existed and many educational psychologists used 'specific learning difficulties' or 'learning disability' to refer to children of average ability (and above) who struggled – for no apparent reason – to acquire literacy (Nicholson and Fawcett in Fawcett 2001: 141; British Psychological Society 1999: 16–17). Theories abound about the biological, cognitive and behavioural factors of dyslexia, giving hope that there may eventually be a scientifically accurate set of criteria to define dyslexia.

- Biological factors may be genetic in origin (Fisher and Smith in Fawcett 2001: 39–44) or the result of neurological abnormalities in brain development causing auditory and cognitive deficits (Galaburda *et al.* 1994, 2006). Evidence gathered from brain imaging techniques (Shaywitz 2007) suggests that dyslexic people process information differently, and much more slowly than the norm.

- Cognitive theories of learning and analysis of dysfunctions have been the focus of many researchers – dyslexia is accepted as a cognitive condition affecting literacy, which can be investigated using psychological assessments (British Psychological Society 1999: 64). Naming-speed affecting reading fluency has been identified as a separate core deficit largely independent of phonological processing – the 'double deficit hypothesis' (Wolf and O'Brien in Fawcett 2001: 130–1).

- Behavioural aspects of dyslexia, and investigation of discrepancies between cognitive ability and literacy levels, may be the starting point for developing effective interventions.

There are many different theories of dyslexia but, since researchers pursue their own particular interests, it is important to set research in context and to remember that current knowledge may be incomplete (Reid 2002).

Working definition of dyslexia

Some definitions of dyslexia are too remote from what is happening in the classroom to be of much practical use to teachers seeking to identify dyslexic characteristics in their students.

The British Psychological Society (1999: 44) produced a working definition focused on literacy learning and a phonological deficit and Snowling (2000: 138) agrees with this definition, asserting that a phonological deficit is 'the proximal cause of dyslexia'.

The British Dyslexia Association (2007) offers a much broader definition, citing the neurobiological origin of dyslexia and listing a number of unexpected difficulties that can affect developing literacy skills:

> Dyslexia is characterised by difficulties with phonological processing, rapid naming, working memory, processing speed and the automatic development of skills that are unexpected in relation to an individual's other cognitive abilities.

Reid (2004: 17) offers a very broad definition of dyslexia and many teachers will find his continuum of characteristics of dyslexia (2004: 5–8) useful when making provision for dyslexic students. He looks beyond definitions and identifies proactive strategies that teachers may use in their daily practice. McKay (2005: 5) describes dyslexia as a 'learning difference which may cause unexpected difficulties' that teachers can identify by observation of learning behaviours.

There is no single, clear definition of dyslexia, no set of symptoms that are always present and no predictable set of circumstances that will always result in dyslexia (Reid in Peer and Reid 2001: 10–11) and the links between theory and practice are not readily accessible by classroom teachers. Successful teaching and learning approaches have often been developed by teachers themselves from observation and experimentation in the classroom. Most secondary teachers are less interested in the debate about the causes and definitions of dyslexia than in learning about *how* dyslexia might affect students' learning in the subject curriculum, and what they can do to minimise its effect in the classroom (Thomson 2007a: 10).

Identification of dyslexia

Describing broad characteristics of dyslexia linked to the processing of information affecting the acquisition of literacy may be a useful starting point for teachers looking to identify students who may be dyslexic. Reid and Fawcett (2004: 3–20), suggest a number of persistent characteristics of dyslexia that might be identified:

- poor use of short- and long-term memory;
- inability to process information at speed;
- lack of automaticity;
- visual inefficiency;
- phonological processing difficulties;
- poor organisation and coordination;
- inability to use meta-cognitive strategies.

Despite the many known indications of dyslexia, there is no single simple manifestation in the secondary subject classroom. There are long lists of signs (BDA 2006a; Dyslexia Scotland 2005a) that subject teachers might use to help identify the likelihood of a student fitting a dyslexic profile. Although it is improbable that any dyslexic student will manifest every indicator on these lists, teachers could reasonably request the school's specialist staff to investigate students who regularly display several of these in class.

General indications of dyslexia

Secondary subject teachers may be the first to recognise that students are experiencing difficulties in the curriculum, and they must not assume that these are known to support staff, parents – or even the students themselves (Thomson 2007a: 7). Effective liaison between subject teachers and the dyslexia specialist is vital for the identification of dyslexia at secondary because:

● Dyslexia is often hidden – perhaps masked by high ability or distracting behaviours – dyslexic students achieve well in some subjects, and teachers assume that poor performance in other areas is due to lack of effort.

● The discrepancy between different aspects of dyslexic performance is often very wide, and some students who experience unexpected difficulties become discouraged, giving up quickly and appearing lazy or lacking concentration.

Sometimes students' difficulties are first revealed at home by changes in attitude and behaviour, especially where homework is involved. Parents may have observed but not recognised characteristics of dyslexia (BDA 2006a) including:

● early speech problems;

● difficulties with shoelaces and ball catching;

● persistent problems telling left from right;

● difficulties with sequences;

● problems with memory;

● comments in school reports about laziness, carelessness, lack of effort.

If these earlier problems reappear or new problems emerge after transfer to secondary school, it would be reasonable for the parent to ask the school to investigate possible dyslexia.

Transition to secondary school

Primary records are passed to secondary schools at transition, so procedures for passing on information about students have already been established. Dyslexic students should be identified and information, including Individualised Educational Programmes and details of any *School Action* or *School Action Plus* interventions, provided in time for the secondary to plan appropriate provision (DfES 2001a: 57).

Profiles of dyslexic students should be available to secondary staff well before the transfer date so that transition programmes and appropriate support may be planned. This profile might include:

- information about test results (and any access arrangements);
- anecdotal evidence re classroom performance;
- information about the student's preferred learning style;
- details of how dyslexia affects access to the curriculum;
- details of successful teaching/learning strategies;
- details of non-curricular achievements;
- parents' comments about out of school behaviours and activities.

(Thomson 2006: 9)

Secondary dyslexia specialists can pass this information to subject colleagues indicating how learning and access to the curriculum might be affected, suggesting strategies to minimise barriers to learning in different subjects by identifying a student's strengths and highlighting areas where support may be required.

Identification of dyslexia during the secondary years

Many secondary teachers assume that any dyslexia will have been identified and assessed at primary, and that relevant information will be passed to them as part of transition arrangements. But there are some aspects of dyslexia that do not become apparent until students begin to experience difficulties within the secondary curriculum (The National Assembly for Wales 2006: 61). This may be due to differences between the primary classroom and the busy secondary school timetable, causing dyslexic problems to emerge – or the move to secondary school has eliminated many of the support strategies that 'hidden' dyslexic students developed at primary to mask that they were having problems. There are some dyslexic difficulties that may not appear until the demands of the secondary subject curriculum outweigh a student's coping strategies. The time aspect of the secondary timetable often creates problems for dyslexic students accustomed to having all the time they need in the primary classroom or a mismatch between a student's apparent ability and the quality (and quantity) of written work may be observed in some subjects.

Case study: Jill, age 12

Jill's dyslexia was identified for the first time after she had transferred to secondary school. She wrote:

I am dyslexic. I must always have been dyslexic, but I didn't know till I went to secondary school.

When I was at primary I knew I was different from the other students but I didn't know why. I learned to read and write just as well as everybody else but over the years I found it increasingly difficult to keep up, though I didn't have any trouble understanding what was going on in the classroom – except for Maths! My strategy at this stage was to copy from my friends. When things got too much for me, I developed 'headaches' and 'sore tummies' and had to go to the nurse to lie down.

By primary 5 I was very worried and I finally told my mum about my difficulties. She was great and went to talk to my teacher who said that I did have a bit of a problem but there was nothing to worry about. I was hurt that my teacher didn't understand but I told mum things were OK but actually, things were getting worse.

During my last year at primary I found it harder to copy from people because they worked much faster – so my spelling took a serious turn for the worse. Even then, the teacher decided I was just more careless and that I wasn't concentrating when doing written work.

I was worried about moving to secondary school, because I didn't know how I would cope with the greater workload, but part of me was relieved I was moving on, because I would be able to leave all the unfinished work behind.

Life at high school was OK at first. I could keep up with most of the work and I didn't fall behind – I just spent hours every night getting Mum's help with homework and I was permanently tired. I kept getting lost in the school building and didn't dare ask to go to the nurse, because I wouldn't know how to find the medical room.

After the first term I started to find it harder to understand things in class and people were getting fed up with having to keep me right all the time. Some of them thought I was boring because I didn't meet them in town or text them – but I thought that if I told them I got lost changing buses and couldn't put numbers into my phone in the right order they would laugh at me. So I just stopped going to school – I would leave home as usual then wait till mum had left for work and go back – and when the school phoned, I pretended to be mum and said I was ill.

I don't know what would have happened if mum hadn't come home unexpectedly and caught me – but she did and it all came out. This time she insisted that I saw the educational psychologist who identified dyslexia very quickly.

—————————

Like Jill, students whose dyslexia was not identified in the primary school probably use successful coping strategies to conceal and compensate for any difficulties, including considerable peer support. Transfer to the secondary school may unintentionally remove important peer support when students are allocated to classes – in Jill's case, the primary teacher suggested that she was separated from certain students because of their habit of chatting and distracting each other – which was actually Jill's strategy for asking for and receiving help.

Sometimes, students may have overcome their dyslexic difficulties to such an extent that the reading demands of certain subjects do not appear to pose particular problems and occasional lapses in spelling or slowness in completing assignments may be the only indications of dyslexia in their written work. As a result, subject teachers may assume that the dyslexia is in some way 'cured' and that a student's dyslexic profile no longer applies. But there is no 'cure' for dyslexia although some people develop very efficient strategies for compensating for their difficulties. Teachers should remain aware that dyslexic difficulties may reappear at any time as the student progresses through the secondary curriculum, especially in stressful situations such as exams (Thomson 2007a: 7).

Impact of multilingualism

Initially, multilingual students may make slow progress in the secondary curriculum, due to limitations in their command of the carrier language and cultural differences, and many schools provide extra support in subject classrooms to improve access to the curriculum.

The processing delay that is evident for all students in the early stages of acquisition of a new language – hear a word, translate it into the 'first' language, understand its meaning and then reverse this process to formulate a response – is similar to the processing delay experienced by many dyslexic students all the time (Reid 2004: 57–9). Bilingual students who continue to exhibit an auditory-verbal processing delay are often considered to be taking longer to develop fluency or perhaps struggling with cultural differences and unfamiliar subject vocabulary, when they are actually demonstrating dyslexic difficulties. The underlying language-processing problems experienced by many dyslexic students may make learning any new language difficult (Schneider and Crombie 2003: 4–5).

Differences between the aural/oral abilities of students who are learning a new language and the level of written work in that language are expected, but reading deficiencies may be more difficult to detect, problems often being linked with unfamiliar vocabulary and cultural differences. Cline and Shamsi (2000: 15) explore evidence that children who are literate in their first language will learn to read more quickly in a second. This places dyslexic learners at a greater disadvantage – they will have to learn to read all over again and, perhaps, repeat the same pattern of difficulties they experienced in their first language.

Case study: Mei, age 13 – bilingual

Although Mei had attended English classes in Hong Kong, her English skills were evaluated as being very limited – she was very slow to respond to spoken language and did not speak, read or write at all in English. Intensive daily English lessons were arranged and a bilingual teaching assistant (TA) was provided to support her in the subject curriculum by translating teacher's instructions and helping with reading and note-taking. It soon became apparent that she was a gifted mathematician, and her only problems in that subject were following the teacher's spoken language and reading maths questions – her notebook was beautifully neat and her mathematical figures clearly legible. She made good progress in most practical subjects once the TA had explained (in Cantonese) what was required. However, she struggled to write anything down in English, her handwriting was illegible and the TA reported that she still did not speak so progress in most subjects was limited.

The EAL teacher, concerned that she might have a specific language impairment, referred Mei to a speech and language therapist but the assessment was inconclusive, possibly due to a cultural bias in the tests used and the need for an interpreter, but the therapist suggested the possibility of dyslexia. The school's dyslexia specialist carried out detailed observations of Mei across the whole curriculum, finding that she demonstrated many behaviours common to dyslexic learners.

A joint strategy was devised – Mei attended the local clinic for speech therapy; the EAL specialist and the bilingual TA continued to support her in class; the dyslexia specialist worked with subject teachers to provide access to a subject curriculum at an appropriate level; and ICT was introduced to help resolve her writing difficulties. This coordinated support worked very well and resulted in Mei reaching a very high standard in maths, computing, graphic design and physics and keeping up with class work in other subjects.

Mei's dyslexia was not fully assessed until application was made for access arrangements for exams – a reader was permitted, along with extra time and computer use (she still did not speak much, so had been unable to use a scribe). Mei achieved very high grades in all subjects except English and eventually was accepted at university to study engineering.

When multilingual learners like Mei fail to make progress in the curriculum as they begin to develop fluency in the new language it should not be assumed that their language status is the only reason. Teachers and psychologists have tended to misdiagnose or ignore dyslexia indicators in multilingual students because of the multiplicity of possible causes for failure to make progress and the risk of a 'false positive' result (Peer and Reid 2000: 5). Schools should look carefully at all aspects of multilingual students' performance in different subjects to establish whether any problems in the classroom arise from special educational needs, including dyslexia (DfES 2001a: 67).

Impact of co-morbid conditions

Dyslexia is often included in a group of developmental disorders – also referred to as specific learning difficulties – but, unlike dyslexia, there is often a clear medical description of symptoms (and treatments) of neuro-developmental syndromes such as dyspraxia and Attention Deficit Hyperactivity Disorder (ADHD) (Elliot *et al.* 2007: 1–2).

The Dyspraxia Foundation (2007) defines dyspraxia as 'an impairment or immaturity of the organisation of movement' but there are often associated problems with language, perception and thought. Developmental dyspraxia (Developmental Coordination Disorder) overlaps with dyslexia to a great extent and milder cases are often identified as dyslexia.

ADHD has been classified (National Institute of Mental Health 2006) as a behavioural and neurological disorder with concentration and impulse control significantly lagging in development when compared to the general population. ADHD often results in difficulties in acquiring literacy and numeracy and students may be identified as dyslexic.

Other conditions may contribute to a student being identified as dyslexic, e.g. long-term school absence or:

- Visual impairment – perhaps linked to refusal to wear corrective lenses causing inability to see the text when reading.

- Hearing problems – 'glue ear' may have hindered auditory perception of sounds and development of phonic skills causing delays in responding to stimuli, similar to dyslexic difficulties (Peer 2005).

- Mild epilepsy/petit mal may result in classroom behaviours – inattention, lack of concentration and gaps in continuity similar to a dyslexic student's losing the place when reading or inability to remember a sequence of instructions.

- Delays or deficits in speech and language development, including pronunciation of words, vocabulary development and understanding of spoken language may be part of a dyslexic profile. A history of dysphasia or an early referral to a speech and language therapist may predict the emergence of dyslexic difficulties at a later stage.

- Clumsy or accident-prone students with impaired gross and fine motor movements may be unable to anticipate movements of others, e.g. when playing team games, similar to dyslexic students' perceptual difficulties causing problems judging speed and distance.

Secondary subject teachers may struggle to distinguish between a number of physical and sensory conditions and specific learning difficulties. The growing *Dyslexia Friendly Schools* initiative (DfES/BDA 2005: 29) promotes strategies developed to support dyslexic students by anticipating their needs and meeting these through inclusive provision.

Referral for investigation

Dyslexia may be difficult for subject teachers to identify, but any mismatch between a student's apparent ability and the quality (and quantity) of written work may be observed. Subject teachers could use a checklist (see **Photocopiable 1.1**, pp. 132–3) to help identify the possibility of dyslexia – if a student demonstrates several of the indicators, referral could be made for investigation and, perhaps assessment. It would be preferable for several non-dyslexic students to be investigated than for one dyslexic student to be missed and left unsupported throughout the secondary years.

Further reading

MILES, T.R. AND MILES, E. (1999) *Dyslexia: A Hundred Years On* (2nd edn), Berkshire: Open University Press.

OTT, P. (1997) *How to Detect and Manage Dyslexia: A Reference and Resource Manual*, Oxford: Heinemann Educational.

UNIVERSITY OF EDINBURGH (2007) *Dyslexia at Transition* [DVDRom], Edinburgh: University of Edinburgh/SITC website at www.dyslexiatransition.org/.

CHAPTER 2

Investigation and assessment of dyslexia in secondary schools

In this chapter, readers will:

- develop awareness of the process of investigating dyslexia in a secondary-age student;

- consider the relative roles of educational psychologists, specialist dyslexia teachers, subject teachers, teaching/learning assistants, parents and students;

- look at case studies to set dyslexia in context;

- trace the process of the investigation of dyslexia from gathering information and classroom observation to assessment and reporting;

- become aware of the range of assessment procedures and materials available.

Investigating dyslexia

A request for dyslexia to be investigated could come from a teacher, a student, parents or a teaching/learning assistant. Many schools have teachers who have been trained to investigate and assess students' dyslexia, so an investigation can begin as soon as parents have been consulted, without the need to involve an external agency.

Role of the special needs/support team

The dyslexia specialist in most schools (DfES 2004: 56–8) is likely to be part of a wider support team, and the whole team may be involved in carrying out the initial investigation of a possible dyslexic profile. The dyslexia specialist may manage the assessment process and carry out standardised testing while other teachers and teaching/learning assistants may gather information from files and colleagues and carry out structured observations of the student in various contexts. Analysing information and interpreting test results may be done at a team meeting prior to issuing a report that identifies strengths and areas of difficulty, relates these to the demands of the subject curriculum, identifying barriers to learning and suggesting strategies for meeting any additional needs.

Role of the subject teacher

Subject teachers play a major role in the identification of students who experience difficulties and assessing barriers to learning in their subject curriculum. Some may routinely refer students for specialist investigation, while others deal with any difficulties themselves, but all should contribute details of a student's progress, identifying strengths or particular difficulties, providing written comments and examples of the student's work, even completing checklists.

Role of teaching/learning assistants

Most schools now use teaching/learning assistants (TAs) in the classroom for a range of duties from providing individual support in class for SEN students to supporting the teacher's delivery of the curriculum. It is important that teachers and TAs play complementary roles, avoiding over-dependence on the TA and consequently depriving students of teacher attention (DfES 2004: 60).

Some TAs play an important part in the investigation of dyslexia. Since few subject teachers have detailed knowledge about the manifestations of dyslexia in the secondary classroom and the impact of these on subject learning, (Peer in Peer and Reid 2001: 3–4) TAs are often able to contribute valuable comments about how students cope in different subjects with different activities and provide insights into their attitudes, behaviour and relationships with peers that may not be picked up by teachers. TAs who work closely with the support team may also be trained to carry out specific tasks during an investigation of dyslexia – such as recording observations of students in different subjects or perhaps completing a skills inventory or checklist.

Many TAs have a closer personal relationship with students than would be possible – or appropriate – for teachers, so they are often able to contribute insights into learning behaviour that would be otherwise missed (Calder 2004).

Case study: Mark, age 11 – behavioural difficulties

Mark's primary school identified his serious behavioural problems and sometimes violent disruption in class. The educational psychologist reported him as being of above average intelligence but uncooperative during the assessment process, reporting that his behaviours were not inconsistent with Oppositional/Defiant Disorder. Extra transition arrangements were made to support his transfer to secondary school and he was included in a group where older students shared their experiences of the school's behaviour policy. He cooperated well throughout the transition programme and it was hoped that the differences between the primary and secondary school settings would help his behaviour to stabilise.

Because of his history of violent outbursts, extra teaching-assistant time was allocated to support him in the curriculum but he had not met the special needs TA during the transition programme. When he was introduced to her on his first day, it was explained that she would be in some of his subject classes to provide support if he needed it. The plan had been to explain about recognising triggers and how he could involve the TA in dealing with these – but his immediate response to the TA was angry and loud. When he eventually calmed down and was able to explain, he said he did not want to be helped by the TA because this would make him look stupid. A compromise was reached – the TA would go to his classes and help out generally with other students – but he would have first call on her support if he began to feel angry.

The TA was asked to observe Mark's learning across the curriculum and note any traits that might contribute to a clearer sense of the source of his anger. However, within the week, Mark had been excluded from school for throwing a book at a teacher, damaging classroom furniture and kicking a hole in a door. Fortunately, the TA had managed to get him out of the classroom without any physical damage to himself or others.

Asked to contribute to a report for a meeting with Mark and his parents to discuss possible arrangements for readmission, the TA commented that the incident had been triggered by the teacher asking Mark to read aloud – he refused, the teacher insisted and his violent outburst followed. She had also observed that when writing was required in subject classes he produced very little, and commented that he acted just like some dyslexic boys she had supported previously. There was no record of standardised scores for reading and spelling because of Mark's refusal to cooperate in the test situation, so any discrepancy was not apparent.

Parents agreed to support these tests and Mark finally admitted that he could not read well and that writing was very hard – he reported that when he told his teacher this at primary, she said to try harder. He did try but was accused of being lazy so he got angry and was sent out of the room – he said he would much rather be thought to be bad than stupid.

The school required investigation of Mark's behaviour and support needs to provide a basis for readmission – or evidence of the need for removal to a special unit. The TA was able to contribute details of her informal observation, and relate these to her experiences with other students, resulting in a reassessment, suggesting dyslexia that had been masked by his disruptive behaviour and could have been missed completely.

Mark's refusal to complete standardised tests meant that his dyslexic difficulties were not initially apparent. During the assessment process he found working with the TA less intimidating and less stressful than working with an unfamiliar educational psychologist and he was able to complete tests that helped diagnose his dyslexia.

Consulting parents and students

SEN and disability legislation (Reid 2004: 94–111) requires that schools involve parents immediately when it is suspected that a student may have special educational needs and their support – and permission – requested for an investigation of dyslexia. The school may request an eye test by an optometrist to rule out any visual impairment as the cause of reading difficulties or parents may be asked to complete a questionnaire or checklist to explore possible dyslexia indicators not usually seen in school.

The SEN Code of Practice (DfES 2001a: 66) requires schools to involve students in planning targets to meet their needs, so any proposed investigation of dyslexia should be discussed with them before any other action is taken. It is important that the implications of dyslexia – including an explanation of what it is – are explained carefully so that students are aware that they are being offered a way to resolve problems they have encountered in the curriculum, not being labelled as low ability or badly behaved. If a student being investigated for dyslexia does not cooperate in all aspects of the assessment process, it is unlikely that an accurate profile will be obtained (see Case study: Mark – behavioural difficulties, p. 13).

Gathering information

Although there are a number of possible approaches to investigation, it is unlikely that anyone would proceed directly to formal psychometric testing – even if referral to an educational psychologist is usual practice or has been specifically requested. The investigation stage of the assessment process will take place in school where trained teachers are able to interpret students' difficulties and behaviours in terms of the demands of the curriculum (Thomson 2007a: 8).

An assessment may start with a review of the student's educational history and the results of any standardised tests previously administered. It is usual practice in secondary schools to ask students' subject teachers to provide information about progress and behaviour in the classroom. If dyslexia indicators are identified in several subjects and the results of the preliminary investigation show inconsistencies, further investigation should be considered.

Classroom observation

Once parental permission for assessment is in place and the results of any sensory testing are known, the specialist teacher may arrange for observation of classroom behaviours to identify features that may be typical of dyslexic students. Peer and Reid (2003: 24–6) offer a detailed framework for observation covering a broad range of areas – or a dyslexia checklist (see p. 129) might be annotated showing a student's demonstration of listed behaviours. Observation should be carried out in a number of different subjects at different times of day at different stages of the lessons. Observers do not have to remain in the same class for a whole lesson – unless there are particular concerns that make this important. Although the class will be aware of the presence of the observer, it is vital that the student being assessed is not identified, even to the subject teacher, since this knowledge will affect the behaviour and attitude of both and may not reflect normal practice. Observations may be carried out by specialist dyslexia teachers who are well equipped to distinguish between dyslexic behaviours and manifestations of other learning difficulties, though some teaching/learning assistants may be already in a position to carry out this task, provided they are given appropriate training.

Recording observations

The first signs of dyslexic difficulties in the secondary subject classroom may be behavioural, so it would be useful to scan and record the student's learning behaviour. **On** or **Off Task** behaviour might be noted:

- **Disruption:** is usually easy to identify, as students' actions result in consequences that interrupt others' work.

- **Talking in class:** On Task behaviour would be asking the page number – while chatting about a movie would be Off Task behaviour.

- **Attention/concentration problems:** it may be difficult to distinguish between On/Off Task behaviour in this area, but observers should be alert to any delays in the student's response to spoken or visual input.

Since classroom observations form part of the evidence in the assessment process, it is important that records are kept (see **Photocopiables 2.1** and **2.2**, pp. 134–5) – including details of activities, e.g. practical lesson, mainly reading/writing activities, and so on – with a brief description of a teacher's delivery style and any support strategies or differentiation in place (Peer and Reid 2003: 27).

Role of the educational psychologist

Kelly and Gray (2000: 84) report that many schools consider that the role of an educational psychologist is to assess individual children and for many years, assessments of dyslexia were carried out by education authorities' psychologists. Although some parents and education authorities are happy to continue this practice, the educational psychologist's role within the school is now understood to be the provision of advice and support. Some of the tasks that would traditionally be associated with the educational psychology service, such as carrying out school-based assessments, are now being undertaken by specialist teachers (DfES 2004: 56).

Specialist teachers have been trained in the administration and interpretation of standardised assessment instruments, and, with their knowledge and experience of the secondary subject curriculum, they are better placed than visiting psychologists to investigate the probability of students' dyslexia and relate this to the curriculum.

The various SEN Codes of Practice that support legislation in the UK place strict time limits for completing assessments and it may be difficult for these to be met if an educational psychologist's heavy case load and extensive other duties have created a long 'waiting list'. In some authorities the specialist teacher and psychological services work together – the teacher carries out the school-based investigation and testing for dyslexia and works with the educational psychologist to interpret the results and make a diagnosis (Northants CC 2006: 3, 6). In other areas psychological services are invited to participate in the assessment process where school-based assessment results are inconsistent or confusing (North Ayrshire Council 2007: 12). Whatever system is in place in an education authority, the identification of a likely dyslexic profile will be best done in the school, and school-based staff will be best placed to translate any diagnosis of dyslexia into provision to meet students' needs in the subject curriculum (Thomson 2007a: 10).

Screening for a dyslexic profile

There are several dyslexia screening tests available that will give teachers a speedy indication of the probability of dyslexia and decisions on whether to investigate further may be based on the results of these, in the context of other information gathered. Some teachers use them in a battery of assessment instruments for diagnosis of a dyslexic profile or to indicate areas for additional testing. Some assessment instruments are complex, taking a long time to administer and evaluate, so many teachers are turning to electronic versions in order to speed up the process and to reduce the fatigue and boredom that students might experience during lengthy testing sessions. Electronic tests have been fully validated and results compared with those obtained using more traditional test instruments (Lucid Research 2003, 2007). The advantages of using electronic assessments are clear, and the fact that many of the complex statistical calculations are performed by the software makes them more attractive to teachers who dread having to consult dense conversion tables to obtain standardised scores.

A diagnosis of dyslexia should not be based on an electronic profile or other formal test results alone and interpretation of these should be considered alongside other information and interactions with the student during the whole assessment process.

Sharing results of assessment

When the results of the assessment process indicate that a student fits a dyslexic profile, the specialist teacher should provide details of this in a report to both the student and parents that relates strengths and difficulties to the subject curriculum and includes possible remediation and support suggestions.

Subject teachers should be made aware of *how* a student's dyslexia is likely to affect learning their subject – and appropriate support strategies suggested (Thomson 2007a: 10). Dyslexia will affect students differently in different subjects, so support provision may vary considerably across the curriculum.

Monitoring and review

Identifying dyslexic profiles and suggesting support strategies for use in the subject curriculum is only the beginning of providing dyslexic students access to an appropriately challenging curriculum. Subject teachers might need help to put some strategies in place, and training opportunities should be identified to equip them to meet the additional needs of dyslexic students in the secondary subject curriculum.

Pupil progress should be reviewed regularly, perhaps measured through target setting in an Individualised Educational Plan where strategies that are additional to or different from the differentiated curriculum provision are recorded with information about:

- short-term targets set for or by the student;
- teaching strategies to be used;
- support provision to be put in place;
- when the plan is to be reviewed;
- success and/or exit criteria.

(DfES 2001a: 5:60, 6:58)

Where students' dyslexia does not require additional differentiation of the key areas of the curriculum but will impact on subject learning, schools may provide a different style of plan – e.g. a Personal Learning Plan (Scottish

Executive 2005: 41) – which will describe support strategies that are additional to or different from what is generally provided and may be either cross curricular or subject specific.

An IEP or other support plan should be reviewed regularly and next steps discussed with the student and the parents (DfES 2001a: 76).

Further reading

CALDER, I. (2004) 'Including Pupils with Dyslexia: How can Classroom Assistants Help?' Paper presented at BDA Conference, University of Warwick, March 2004, retrieved 14 March 2007 www.bdainternationalconference. org/2004/presentations/mon_s6_b_5.shtml.

LUCID RESEARCH (2003) *Fact Sheet 21*, LASS Junior and LASS Secondary case studies, retrieved 17 July 2007 www.lucid-research.com/documents/fact sheets/FS21_LASScasestudies.pdf.

Classroom management of dyslexia

In this chapter, readers will:

- become aware of the general characteristics of dyslexia;

- begin to identify barriers to learning across the curriculum;

- examine the implications of dyslexia for classroom management;

- consider strategies teachers might adopt to deal with the impact of dyslexia on students' classroom behaviour, learning styles, organising ability and self-esteem;

- look at case studies to set dyslexic students' classroom behaviour in context;

- review examples of support strategies.

Some general characteristics of dyslexia

Dyslexia is *not* the result of poor motivation, emotional disturbance, sensory impairment or lack of opportunities, although it may occur alongside any of these. Since one person in ten is thought to be dyslexic to some degree, some secondary students will require additional support in the curriculum (Peer in Peer and Reid 2001: 3–6).

Dyslexic students constantly meet barriers to learning across the curriculum and may become discouraged very quickly due to lack of initial success in subject classes resulting in teachers assuming that they are inattentive or lazy, when they may actually be making much more effort than their classmates. Pupils whose dyslexia has not been recognised or fully understood will probably not be successful learners, so are unlikely to be motivated to learn (Peer in Peer and Reid 2001: 5), and the experience of success may be rare, if not totally absent (Houston 2002: 25). In addition to struggling with literacy issues, dyslexic students often:

- lack self-confidence;

- appear to avoid set work;

- are very disorganised;

- lack stamina;

- have a poor self image.

(Thomson 2007b: 8)

Although each dyslexic student has an individual learning style and profile of strengths and difficulties, experience of working with other dyslexic students may help teachers identify barriers to learning in their subjects. Generally, dyslexic students perform better orally than in reading and writing activities – a dyslexic student may understand a teacher's presentation of a topic but be unable to follow written instructions to complete class activities; handwriting is often laboured and deteriorates into illegibility; written work may be characterised by weak spelling and poorly sequenced ideas. Dyslexic students often appear restless and unable to concentrate or easily tired, inattentive and uncooperative. They may be talented in performance-related activities or gifted academically (Thomson 2006: 30) – they may be superb athletes, have good problem-solving skills or strongly developed spatial awareness, but they often underachieve, quickly losing interest and appearing bored or becoming frustrated and disruptive (Thomson 2006: 21 for lists of underachieving behaviours; and **Photocopiable 3.1**, p. 136).

Implications for classroom management

In any subject classroom there will be a wide variety of learning styles, barriers to learning and support needs for which provision must be made, so it is important for subject teachers to recognise and respond effectively to the learning needs of students, providing additional support when necessary (Given and Reid 1999: 81–3). Many teaching and learning strategies appropriate for dyslexic students that take account of a range of strengths and learning differences, are effective for all students (McKay in Reid and Fawcett 2004: 231–3).

Barriers to learning across the curriculum

In the classroom, students with dyslexia face not only problems caused by dyslexia, but also experience feelings linked to self-esteem that may contribute to lack of progress (Peer and Reid 2003: 41). Teachers' recognition of possible barriers to learning that require additional support provision, and good classroom management of these are essential for dyslexic students' effective learning. The impact of dyslexia varies from one student to another and may apply only to some aspects of performance – underpinning literacy difficulties combined with lack of self-confidence may result in students apparently making little effort, when they are actually struggling to process the text required for the task set. Low-quality written work may lead to assumptions about attitude and effort – some dyslexic students complete written assignments to the best of their ability, only to find their work returned with negative comments about presentation or lack of effort because of the discrepancy between their comprehension of subject material and their ability to write legibly or spell consistently (McKay in Reid and Fawcett 2004: 224).

Dyslexia is often hidden by ability. In some subjects dyslexic students perform very well, and, as a result, their additional needs may not be observed by the teacher for some time (Dodds and Thomson 1999). Some-times subject ability is masked by dyslexia – a student is performing at the expected level but is actually limited by underpinning dyslexic difficulties and the teacher does not identify a need to introduce additional support that would allow the demonstration of actual ability (Montgomery 2003: 8). Teachers should take care when developing differentiated materials that the tasks set for students with dyslexia are appropriate to their ability level. Differentiation should lead to the curriculum being presented in a more accessible format but teaching and learning resources and activities must not be over-simplified in the process (Fawcett in Peer and Reid 2001: 270).

Dyslexic students encounter barriers to learning across the whole curriculum so it is important for subject teachers to remain aware that dyslexia may prevent them from producing work that matches their level of understanding of the subject curriculum. A subject curriculum that encourages students to be active learners, using materials that are presented and sequenced in a way that takes account of the range of attainment is less likely to create problems for students with dyslexia.

Dealing with classroom behaviour

Some dyslexic students' inability to remember spoken instructions or process written directions may be interpreted as lack of attention or indiscipline when they ask classmates for a page number or what to do next. Teachers might anticipate such problems – e.g. always write page and question numbers on the board – and should evaluate the likely impact on dyslexic students of class activities set and provide alternatives to ensure their inclusion and enable them to complete set work.

Case study: Roberto, age 12 – hidden dyslexia

Roberto's first secondary school report raised concerns that his lack of progress in some subjects might be linked to his bilingualism. Records showed that his reading was slightly below average but his maths was well above average and there was no suspicion that he might have any specific difficulties. A special needs learning assistant was asked to 'shadow' him in subject classes to see if an explanation for the lack of progress could be identified.

The learning assistant noted that he was habitually late for subject classes, but always had a 'good' excuse – often the same one repeated throughout the day to different teachers. He appeared attentive in class, making good oral contributions, but when writing tasks were set, Roberto would take a very long time organising his desk before picking up his pencil to write the date. The pencil would immediately break, so he would proceed to sharpen it – often until it was little more than a stump – wasting a considerable amount of time.

When he eventually made his way back to his seat he would rearrange his desk before starting to write; at this point he would often ask the teacher – or a classmate – to remind him what the task was. The observer noted that even when he started to write, he erased most of his work, resulting in very little writing being produced before the time was up.

He went through the same ritual in every subject, though – if the writing task was a long one – Roberto often asked permission to leave the room – for any one of a number of reasons. In one class, the teacher refused to allow him to sharpen his pencil and gave him a pen – which turned out to be a mistake, as it resulted in the complete destruction of the pen, with ink everywhere, covering Roberto, his exercise book and his desk. Another teacher refused to allow him to leave the room, so he put his head on his desk and closed his eyes for the rest of the lesson. Even when ICT was used for writing, he managed to exit the program or 'crash' the computer without saving any work.

With different teachers every lesson, Roberto's behaviour was not picked up as an avoidance strategy at first, although his maths teacher was clearly prepared for it, and had a box of sharp pencils ready on her desk – she assumed this was Roberto's way of trying to avoid having to show his working – not unusual in the maths class.

His spelling was tested and was found to be nearly four years behind. When attempts were made to collect a sample of continuous writing, he broke his pencil (new ones were instantly supplied) and rubbed a hole in the paper, removing what he had just written. After 15 minutes, his finished piece was two lines of tiny, illegible writing.

Parents requested an assessment to find out what the problem was and a dyslexic profile was soon identified. Support strategies were developed – the most immediately effective being the use of a recorder to dictate his work – teachers either accepted this in place of writing or it was transcribed for marking.

When dyslexic students like Roberto are unable to participate in set work, they often appear to make little or no attempt to begin, talking to classmates, or concentrating on personal concerns instead of settling down to work – considered by teachers to be an indication of laziness or disaffection (Thomson 2007b: 10). In order to check that instructions are fully understood, teachers could ask dyslexic students to repeat them aloud or encourage students to discuss the nature of tasks before starting individual work. The level of concentration and effort needed for 'normal' class activities may cause fatigue in dyslexic students making them excessively tired, so teachers might vary activities so that they become less fatigued or build-in mini-breaks to allow them to rest briefly.

Many dyslexic students are disorganised or forgetful of equipment and homework – even turning up in class at the wrong time (Fawcett in Peer and Reid 2001: 270). The use of equipment checklists and personal timetables with deadlines clearly marked will support dyslexic students' development of personal strategies for coping with the complexities of the secondary curriculum.

Coping strategies

- Talking to classmates instead of settling to work;

- appearing not to pay attention (struggling to process spoken language);

- playing the 'class clown' to divert attention from dyslexic difficulties;

- being disorganised or forgetful;

- excessive fatigue, feeling unwell.

Support strategies

- Check whether students are seeking clarification of instructions;

- encourage students to discuss the nature of tasks set;

- check that instructions are fully understood – repeat these;

- encourage restless students to settle using humour/endless patience;

- model checklists and provide timetables with deadlines clearly shown;

- structure lesson pace and activities to allow rests.

Point to remember

All students are more willing to consult the person next to them than ask the teacher when they are unsure of something. Pupils being asked for help by dyslexic classmates often benefit from the opportunity to talk about the work, and their own understanding may be clarified and their attention focused by having the chance to explain something to another student.

Different learning styles

All students have preferred learning styles and these affect the efficiency with which they learn. Pupils with dyslexia are less able than their classmates to cope when the teaching input is delivered in a style that is different from their individual preference (Given and Reid 1999: 15–16). McKay (2005: 114–18) refers to 'comfort zones' of learning preferences, identifying many dyslexic students' preference for visual and kinaesthetic styles and the need for them to become more comfortable with text and language. Dyslexic students may find themselves adopting different approaches to learning different subjects, depending on teachers' preferred styles of lesson delivery, resulting in unexpected attainment or lack thereof in different subjects, e.g. they may make excellent progress in a subject where a teacher chooses to teach using mind maps and encourages students to develop these, but may be unable to progress beyond the basics in a subject where they are expected to take personal notes and generate extended written pieces.

It is important that teachers explore the preferred learning styles of all students and both adjust their delivery of the curriculum and support students' development of competence in all learning styles in order to ensure that their subjects are accessible to all. Some dyslexic students struggle to understand new concepts and have difficulty processing new subject vocabulary and therefore may meet barriers to accessing text materials or to production of written work linked to this. Parents could be involved and new subject vocabulary lists sent home with advance information about new topics so that dyslexic students are familiar with new terminology when it is used in the classroom and are therefore less likely to become confused. Many dyslexic students are unable to listen and take notes at the same time or to copy from a board, screen or book so teachers could provide templates or copies of class notes in an accessible format – e.g. large print versions. Drawing or completing diagrams with labels may be particularly challenging for some dyslexic students and it might be appropriate for copies of these to be issued – a useful way of 'creating' extra time for dyslexic students to complete other set work.

Point to remember

Dyslexic students may take three to four times longer to complete the same assignment as classmates.

Support strategies

- Multi-sensory teaching – visual aids interspersed with activity;

- provide opportunities to practice using new terminology;

- present information in a variety of ways – charts and diagrams, mind maps, and so on;

- issue only one instruction at a time;

- create opportunities for student discussion;

- allow extra time for completion of set work;

- teach dyslexic students everything directly and explicitly.

Dyslexic students can make good progress in the subject curriculum and are often able to cope well with most set tasks but teachers should remain aware that it may require more time and effort for them to achieve the same results as classmates.

Managing poor organising ability

Poor organisational skills are often exacerbated by an inability to remember sequences of events, tasks and instructions, a tendency to forget books and work to be handed in and failure to meet deadlines for assignments or to complete tasks on time.

Indications of poor organisation skills

- Difficulties taking notes in class;

- inability to complete tasks on time;

- forever searching in bags for books and equipment;

- problems setting work out in an acceptable – even legible – format;

- losing work – in notebooks, files and even on computers;

- difficulties with organisation and completion of homework;

- inability to remember sequences of events, tasks.

When planning lessons, subject teachers might structure tasks for dyslexic students and help them to prioritise – especially when problems are associated with homework. Teachers should monitor the correct use of the homework diary and involve parents, e.g. accepting homework scribed by parents or in an alternative format to writing (Fawcett in Peer and Reid 2001: 270–1).

Point to remember

The organisation difficulties of dyslexic students will extend beyond the classroom into all aspects of living and what is observed in the classroom may be only the tip of a very large iceberg.

Support strategies

- Give intended learning outcomes at the start of each lesson;
- summarise what has been covered at the end of each lesson;
- create opportunities to rehearse/practice – e.g. terminology, tasks;
- provide copies of class notes or a skeleton structure;
- provide models of layout of work and issue worksheets/templates for completion;
- do not automatically set unfinished reading or writing as homework;
- help students to devise personal methods to improve sequencing and memory;
- structure tasks for dyslexic students and highlight priorities.

Dealing with the effects of fatigue

Dyslexia is not only a series of difficulties – it includes a range of specific abilities. A dyslexic student may be creative, artistic, sporting or orally very able and knowledgeable and the disparity between the difficulties and abilities is often noted in a student's profile (Montgomery 2003: 7–9; McKay 2005: 15). The huge effort required by many dyslexic students to complete an ordinary task that others can tackle automatically may cause unanticipated fatigue.

Dyslexic students may start a task well but there is often a rapid deterioration of the quality of work, especially when writing. Setting short, well-defined tasks, varying the types of tasks and setting time limits for the duration of activities may help prevent some dyslexic students spending so much time on initial tasks that they fail to participate in the rest of the lesson and help to teach them how to pace themselves.

Many dyslexic students appear to do everything the long way – concentration is easily lost and they are unable to pick up from where they left off, often having to start all over again, leading them to become restless or disruptive to draw attention away from their difficulties.

Indicators of fatigue

- Quality of work deteriorates quickly;
- loss of concentration leading to restlessness or disruption;
- complaints of minor ailments – asking to leave the room;
- lack of automaticity in ordinary activities;
- having to start at the beginning – being unable to join in at any point;

- inability to keep up with the class so misses bits out;
- failure to take note of homework.

Point to remember

If clearly defined targets are set, showing the intermediate steps to be completed in an activity, dyslexic students may learn how to monitor their progress and pace themselves appropriately.

Support strategies

- Set short, well-defined tasks;
- vary the types of tasks set;
- set time limits for completion of tasks;
- define targets/intended outcomes clearly;
- teach students to pace themselves;
- devise 'shortcuts' to reduce volume of writing;
- make sure that homework is written down correctly.

Coping with students' poor self-image

Pupils with dyslexia are acutely aware of their problems and may overreact to casual comments and general remarks made by teachers and take everything personally (Thomson 2007b: 13).

Case study: Emily, age 12 – poor self-image

At the beginning of my second year at secondary school, I was starting to find it hard to understand in some classes and I managed to persuade myself that I had a hearing impairment! I had problems following what my history teacher said at the best of times (he had a very funny accent) and one winter day when I had the sniffles it was worse than ever. I asked the person next to me what the teacher had said, but he was behind me and heard – and he asked me if I was deaf – so I said 'Yes'.

Things moved fast after that – my parents were called in and I was taken off to have my ears examined. I actually ended up going to the hospital and then to a special unit for hearing tests. The tests using the machines at the special unit were a bit more complex than I had bargained for, so my deafness 'miraculously' cleared up. In my own defence I have to point out that I did have a cold and was not hearing well at the time.

I expected the next step would be having my head examined – but my parents had been worried about the time I spent on homework even before my 'deaf' episode, so after my hearing was given the all clear, they asked for a full assessment of my difficulties.

I was tested within a week and the results clearly showed that I am dyslexic – my reading is inaccurate and my spelling was at the seven-year-old level (it's not much better now). But the relief was enormous! I had actually started to wonder if I was a bit of a nutcase, but I finally felt vindicated – there really was something wrong with me – I hadn't been imagining things! Now things would get better, I thought . . .

Emily's relief at finding out that she had an identifiable condition is typical of the low self-esteem of most dyslexic students who may adopt a number of self-defeating coping strategies (Hales in Peer and Reid 2001: 237). Teachers should offer encouragement and support for all activities and praise effort as well as work well done. Where writing is a problem, teachers should accept and praise oral contributions and encourage alternatives to writing such as drawings or charts. Dyslexic students themselves are often disappointed at the poor quality and quantity of their work, despite their efforts, and they may adopt an inappropriate attitude in class to hide their frustration at this. They may become too tired to keep up the level of alertness and forward planning needed to sustain the coping strategies and feel humiliated if their difficulties become obvious to their classmates.

Indicators of low self-esteem/poor self-image

- Perception of themselves as failures;

- reluctance to attempt anything new;

- disappointment at a poor return for effort;

- humiliation as difficulties lead to embarrassment;

- despair, exhaustion and inability to employ coping strategies.

Point to remember

Subject teachers should remain alert for difficult situations for dyslexic students and be ready to defuse any potentially embarrassing circumstances.

Support strategies

- Remain aware of dyslexic learning differences;

- anticipate potential difficulties when planning classroom activities;

- praise effort as well as work well done;

- mark on content not presentation of work;

- suggest new ways of coping with dyslexia in the subject context.

Those dyslexic students who have overcome their reading difficulties to some extent may cope with the literacy demands of some subjects and poor spelling and a slow work rate may be the only indications of dyslexia in their class work. As a result, teachers may assume that students have overcome their dyslexia and it will not return. No matter how efficient a dyslexic student's coping strategies are, the difficulties linked to their dyslexia may re-appear at any time in the secondary curriculum and teachers should monitor the possible barriers to learning implicit in the subject curriculum (Dyslexia Action 2005). Subject teachers should remain aware of the individual strengths and weaknesses of dyslexic students and take account of these when planning lessons in order to minimise barriers to learning and achievement and create opportunities for them to experience success.

Subject teachers' use of effective support strategies (see **Photocopiable 3.2**, pp. 137–8) that anticipate barriers to learning and attainment in the subject curriculum can result in dyslexic students' first taste of success.

Further reading

DYSLEXIA SCOTLAND (2006) *Dyslexia: Suggestions for Teachers*, www.dyslexiascotland.org.uk/documents/Dyslexia%20%20Suggestions%20for%20Teachers.pdf.

MELLERS, C. (2000) *Identifying and Supporting the Dyslexic Child*, Desktop Publications www.ic-online.co.uk/em/Detail/it080003.htm.

CHAPTER 4

Framework of support for dyslexic pupils in secondary schools

In this chapter, readers will:

- review and compare Disability and Special Educational Needs and Dyslexia Legislation and Guidance across the UK;

- examine the structures of support for dyslexic pupils at education authority and school level;

- develop awareness of the role of the school in meeting the needs of dyslexic pupils through School Action and School Action Plus, Staged Intervention and the 'Dyslexia Friendly' schools initiative;

- consider the roles of psychological services, specialist teachers and subject teachers in carrying out the duties required by the legislation.

Legislation

The Salamanca Statement (UNESCO 1994) drew attention to the fact that many children experience learning difficulties at some point in school and indicated the responsibility of education services to make effective provision to help all children achieve their potential, taking into account their unique characteristics, interests, abilities and learning needs.

In UK legislation and initiatives (Table 4.1) the 1993 Education Act (England & Wales) required the development of a Code of Practice for meeting Special Educational Needs. The rights and duties in the 1993 Act were consolidated into the 1996 Education Act then amended by the Special Educational Needs and Disability Act 2001 to include:

- a stronger right for children with SEN to be educated at mainstream schools;

Table 4.1

Summary of UK disability and special educational needs legislation and dyslexia guidance

England and Wales	Wales	Scotland	Northern Ireland
The Children Act **1989** (England and Wales) **Disability Discrimination Act 1995** Amended by Part 2 of the Special Educational Needs and Disability Act 1995 The Education Act **1996**, (amended by the SENDA 2001)	**1999** Shaping the Future for Special Education – an Action Programme for Wales	Education (Scotland) Act **1980** Education (Scotland) Act **2001**	**1996** Education (Northern Ireland) Order **1998** Code of Practice on the Identification and Assessment of Special Educational Needs
1997–2002 The National Literacy and Numeracy Strategies	**2001** Special Educational Needs Code of Practice for Wales	**1995** The Children (Scotland) Act	**2002** Dyslexia Task Group Report
2001 DfES The Special Educational Needs Code of Practice	**2002** Education (Special Educational Needs) (Wales) Regulations	**1998** SOEID Professional Practice in Meeting Special Educational Need – A Manual of Good Practice	**2005** Special Educational Needs and Disability (Northern Ireland) Order (SENDO)
2001 DfES SEN Toolkit	**2002** DRC Code of Practice for Schools (England and Wales)	**2000** The Standards in Scotland's Schools etc. Act	**2005** Article 41 of Chapter IV of Part III of SENDO
2001 Inclusive Schooling – Children with SEN	**2003** Handbook of Good Practice for Children with Special Educational Needs	**2002** The Education (Disability Strategies and Pupils' Educational Records) (Scotland) Act	**2006** Supplement to Code of Practice on the Identification and Assessment of Special Educational Needs
2001 DfES Guidance to support pupils with dyslexia and dyscalculia	**2006** Inclusion and Pupil Support National Assembly for Wales Circular No. 47/2006	**2004** The Education (Additional Support for Learning) (Scotland) Act	**2006** The Equality Commission for Northern Ireland Disability Discrimination Code of Practice for Schools
2002 DRC Code of Practice for Schools (England and Wales)	**2007** Children in Wales Interim Report of the Dyslexia Rapporteur Group	**2005** Scottish Executive Supporting Children's Learning (ASfL Code of Practice)	**2007** Commencement No. 1 (Amendment to 2005 (SENDO) Order (Northern Ireland))
2003 The National Literacy Strategy		**2006** Learning and Teaching Scotland Focusing on Inclusion: a Paper for Professional Reflection	
2004 Removing Barriers to Achievement		**2008** HMIe Review of Educational Provision for Children with Dyslexia in Scotland	
2004 Skills for Life: Framework for Understanding Dyslexia			
2008 Say No to Failure Interim Report			
2009 Rose Review of Dyslexia due in 2009			

- new duties on Local Education Authorities to provide parents of children with SEN advice, information and a means of resolving disputes;

- a duty on schools to consult parents about special educational provision;

- a right for schools to request a statutory assessment of a child.

There are differences in legislation across the UK – each country now has its own unique Code of Practice that reflects differences in local educational systems – SEN in England, Wales and Northern Ireland; Additional Support for Learning (ASL) in Scotland. The various Codes of Practice are broadly similar in content, though only Northern Ireland includes advice on provision linked to dyslexia (DENI 1996: 71–3). The Scottish Executive (2005: 36) provides case studies that illustrate various support needs including one for a dyslexic child.

The Disability Rights Commission places a 'reasonable adjustments' duty on schools requiring them to take reasonable steps to ensure that pupils are not placed at a substantial disadvantage or treated less favourably for a reason relating to their disability and uses case studies to indicate discriminatory practice that might impact on dyslexic learners (DRC 2002a: 34, 40, 44; 2002b: 10).

The Education Act 1996 defines special educational needs as 'a learning difficulty which calls for special educational provision to be made' describing provision as 'additional to or otherwise different from provision that is normally available'. The National Assembly for Wales (2006: 19) extended this to include pupils who have additional learning needs who have not been identified as SEN or disabled.

Reid (2004: 110) reports the impact of litigation on the identification and support for dyslexic children in the USA and Canada as well as the UK as resulting in a more constructive approach by governments. Since dyslexia can result in pupils struggling to access the secondary curriculum at an appropriate level, the need to make reasonable adjustments to avoid placing them at a disadvantage may have far-reaching consequences for secondary schools – and the dispute-resolution procedures outlined in the various Codes of Practice may cause teachers to reflect on classroom practice and their delivery of the curriculum.

Structures of support for dyslexic pupils at secondary school

Education authorities

Under UK legislation (Table 4.1), the various education authorities/boards are required to publish policies for meeting the needs of pupils who have disabilities and/or Special Educational Needs; only the DENI Code (1996: 71–3) includes an outline of provision for dyslexic pupils.

The Codes for England and Wales recommend that schools and local education authorities adopt a graduated approach for the identification and assessment of SEN and match provision to children's needs through School Action (DfES 2001a: 68–9) and School Action Plus (DfES 2001a: 71–2). Scotland and Northern Ireland recommend a staged approach built around discrete stages of intervention that seek to anticipate difficulties and resolve them as early as possible with the least intrusive course of action (DENI 1996: 22–4; SEED 2005: 26–7).

Some local authorities have produced separate policy documents on disability, SEN and inclusion, while others have combined these into a single publication (Reid *et al.* 2005: 204). Stockport Council (2006: 6) provides a useful table illustrating the overlap of SEN and disability, showing *mild* dyslexia as SEN but *significant* dyslexia as both SEN and a disability. Angus Council (2006: 153–4) provides operational/procedural advice and information, showing staged intervention in some detail but makes no mention of dyslexia.

Perhaps recognising that dyslexic pupils are likely to form the biggest single 'disability' group in schools, some education authorities have produced separate policies/guidance on dyslexia. The Milton Keynes Council (2003) *Dyslexia Policy*, developed by a working party of psychologists and teachers in consultation with parents and voluntary agencies, forms part of their guidance to assist schools in meeting the needs of children with SEN. The Northamptonshire *Guidelines on Dyslexia* (2006: 3, 6, 7) describes practice and looks at identification and intervention, specifying the roles of schools, the additional needs team and educational psychology service and other agencies as regards dyslexia. North Ayrshire Council (2007) published a jargon-free parents' booklet that explains their procedures for assessing and supporting dyslexia.

The National Assembly for Wales (2006: 41–4) provides a checklist of questions for consideration by authorities to help them evaluate the nature and quality of their provision, and to further develop inclusive strategies. But authority-level support for dyslexia should go beyond evaluating school-based provision to developing a local framework for meeting the needs of dyslexic pupils, perhaps providing a template for schools to follow when designing support provision. The North–South Ireland Dyslexia Task Group (DENI 2002: 59) recommended the development of a Good Practice Guide for schools and parents. This has been taken forward by the voluntary sector, working with individual schools.

Any local authority framework for dyslexia should set out clear expectations and guidelines for schools – and support services – that describe support for initiatives within individual schools and gives details of resources available – including ICT – to support dyslexic pupils and of the provision of relevant professional-development opportunities in dyslexia for all school staff.

Many barriers can stand in the way of dyslexic pupils' access to appropriate education and support and the help they receive often depends on an education authority's published policy. This should draw upon the best existing practice within schools with input from parents, pupils, current research, psychological services and other agencies. Key aspects of this should be strategies for:

- early intervention – to ensure that children who have dyslexic difficulties receive the help they need as soon as possible;

- removing barriers to learning – by raising all teachers' awareness of dyslexia and embedding inclusive practice in every school;

- raising expectations and achievement – by developing teachers' skills to develop strategies for meeting the needs of dyslexic pupils and delivering an appropriate curriculum.

Role of the school

Within the context of national and local policy, every secondary school should identify issues around possible barriers to learning that dyslexic pupils might encounter in the curriculum, and link these to a framework of support designed to minimise them. This framework may form the basis of a school policy on dyslexia that also provides information for parents and pupils and outlines measures already in place within the school. The school's arrangements for the identification and assessment of dyslexia should be included along with details of specialist staff, perhaps naming the member of staff responsible for managing provision for dyslexic pupils (Houston 2002: 4).

Whether or not they have a separate policy for dyslexia, all secondary schools should have systems/procedures in place to ensure that staff, parents and pupils have access to information about the nature of dyslexia and the provision available within the school. There should be a pro-active whole-school approach to identifying pupils' needs and meeting these, such as the Dyslexia Friendly Schools initiative.

'Dyslexia Friendly' schools

Many schools and authorities, in partnership with voluntary dyslexia organisations, have taken the decision to become 'Dyslexia Friendly'. The *Dyslexia Friendly LEAs Initiative* (DfES/BDA 2005) carries a BDA Quality Mark to promote excellent practice by an authority as it carries out its role of supporting and challenging its schools to improve accessibility to learning.

Becoming Dyslexia Friendly requires significant commitment from a school, requiring participation from all teachers and other school staff, parents and pupils, involving evaluation and review of the implementation of school policies. Each Dyslexia Friendly school must have a teacher who is trained in dyslexia and all school policies must reflect good practice in relation to dyslexia. All staff must be aware of strategies and resources that support pupils with dyslexia and use these in curriculum delivery so that the pupils are not disadvantaged in any way – they should:

- recognise that the negative effect of stress on pupils with dyslexia will impact on their learning and their emotional well-being;

- value the individual, praise effort and achievement and promote strengths;

- seek opportunities for continuing professional development on dyslexia.

While a dyslexia-friendly school environment would benefit all pupils (Ofsted 1999: 6), the vulnerability of individual dyslexic pupils must not be ignored and any additional support needs must be met (Johnston in Reid and Fawcett 2004: 253).

School Action and School Action Plus

School Action

When a pupil is identified as dyslexic, subject teachers and the support team should consider interventions that are additional to or different from the school's usual differentiated curriculum and strategies (DfES 2001a: 74). Triggers for intervention through School Action (DfES 2001a: 74–5) may be teachers' concerns that a pupil:

- makes little or no progress even when teaching approaches are targeted on identified areas of weakness;

- shows signs of difficulty in literacy or mathematics that result in poor attainment in some curriculum areas;

- presents persistent emotional and/or behavioural difficulties that do not respond to the school's usual behaviour management techniques.

Further assessment of the pupil's particular strengths and weaknesses should be arranged, while individual subject teachers should take responsibility for devising support strategies and identifying appropriate methods of access to the curriculum. All staff should be involved in providing support for pupils through School Action.

School Action Plus (DfES 2001a: 77)

When pupils fail to make adequate progress through School Action, the school may request help from external services – School Action Plus. Outside specialists can play an important part in the identification of dyslexia and in advising schools on effective provision, acting as consultants and delivering advice and training on teaching and learning strategies. At the secondary level, School Action Plus may be triggered if a dyslexic pupil continues to:

- make little or no progress despite School Action interventions;

- work at levels substantially below that expected of pupils of a similar age;

- experience difficulty in developing literacy and mathematics skills;

- demonstrate emotional or behavioural difficulties that interfere with both the class and the pupil's own learning, despite an individualised programme.

External services may also be approached when pupils have ongoing difficulties that cause substantial barriers to learning, require additional specialist equipment or the direct intervention by a specialist service.

Staged Intervention (DENI 1996: 14–24; SEED 2005: 27)

Secondary subject teachers may be the first to identify the additional needs of dyslexic pupils. Stage 1 support begins when concerns are expressed to the school's support team who make an initial assessment of support needs in consultation with parents and provide advice on additional support measures.

Stage 2 is similar to School Action – and begins when a subject teacher is not satisfied with a pupil's progress and the need for intensive action is identified. Investigation of dyslexia may take place at this stage and a detailed support plan developed, outlining the nature of the pupil's dyslexic difficulties and the additional support provision required. This may take the form of an Individual Education Plan (DfES 2001a: 75–7) or a Personal Learning Plan (SEED 2005: 41–2).

If progress is not satisfactory with Stage 2 support in place, additional expertise should be sought and the pupil should move to Stage 3, which is equivalent to School Action Plus. It is particularly important to involve parents in any decision as Stage 3 involves referral to external specialists, e.g. the area support team or Educational Psychologist. External specialists may work with a pupil directly or may act in an advisory capacity, supporting subject teachers in implementing an education plan, or they may recommend additional specialist support. External specialists might revise support strategies implemented in the classroom by subject teachers and ensure a coordinated approach – with additional support and resources – that takes account of previous difficulties.

Concerns about lack of progress with Stage 3 support could trigger Stage 4 – referral of the pupil, e.g. to an educational psychologist – for formal assessment to clarify the degree and nature of dyslexic difficulties and for advice on other services available. In Scotland, Stage 4 diverges from the rest of the UK – where statements of SEN might be opened at this point – by requiring consideration of whether a Coordinated Support Plan might be appropriate (SEED 2005: 47–72). Dyslexic pupils would not normally qualify for these unless they had additional impairments being treated by other agencies.

Psychological services role

Training opportunities for teachers to become dyslexia specialists are available at most universities and teacher training centres, including distance learning via the Open University and the Hornsby Centre – leading to the award of post graduate certificates, diplomas and Master of Education degrees, accredited by the BDA. These courses have been taken up by large numbers of teachers, enabling them to take up duties in the assessment and support of dyslexia that had previously been the remit of educational psychologists.

Educational psychologists' training is to apply psychology to promote the attainment and healthy emotional development of all pupils. When researching the scope and balance of work of educational psychology services in England, Kelly and Gray (2000: 4–6) found that their increasing involvement in the process of statutory assessment of special educational needs took up so much time that they were unable to undertake fully working with schools to improve provision. Consultation and problem solving are seen as important aspects of educational psychology services' work in the future although they will have a continuing role in supporting schools and working with children with special educational needs. The Joint Council for Qualifications' (2006: 36–7) acceptance of reports by accredited dyslexia teachers for making access arrangements for examinations, relieved educational psychologists of a task that had seriously reduced their capacity to offer a full range of services to some schools.

The educational psychologists' role as regards dyslexia in schools has now become:

- evaluation of research and advice regarding developments;

- support for schools in the development of assessment and support systems;

- provision of training opportunities for teachers;

- providing in-depth assessment and follow-up where a pupil's dyslexia is severe/complex.

Role of the SEN/support team

In mainstream secondary schools the SEN Coordinator (Principal Teacher Support for Learning in Scotland) is usually responsible for the operation of the school's SEN policy and for coordination of the provision made for individual pupils.

The SEN Toolkit (DfES 2001b: Section 5) offers guidance to support teachers on strategies for supporting a pupil's progress and about recording interventions in the IEP – *additional to* or *different from* the curriculum provision for all pupils:

- three to four short-term targets in literacy, mathematics, behaviour/social skills;

- details of teaching strategies to be used;

- support provision/resources/equipment to be put in place;

- time-scale/outcomes;

- success criteria.

Although School Action (Stage 2) provision might include the deployment of extra staff to provide individual support for a pupil, it is more likely that different learning materials, special equipment and group support will be introduced and related professional guidance provided to help teachers develop effective ways of overcoming barriers to learning and sustaining effective teaching (DfES 2001a: 71). The school's dyslexia specialist is likely to have speedy access to authority support services for advice about strategies and provision of equipment or for staff-training opportunities, and this may make it possible to provide effective intervention to support dyslexic pupils without the need for ongoing input from external agencies. Although School Action Plus (Stage 3) planning may involve outside specialists, delivery of support remains the responsibility of subject teachers, with the strategies specified implemented in the classroom setting.

Role of secondary subject teachers

All teachers should expect to teach children with special educational needs, therefore the availability of support must be made clear and procedures put in place designed to enable pupils to understand their difficulties and provide them with the means to compensate for these (DfES 2001a: 65).

In secondary schools there may be an expectation that specialist teachers will provide all support for all dyslexic pupils, but all teachers should see themselves as responsible for removing barriers to learning and developing support strategies for dyslexic pupils within the subject curriculum. Secondary school support for dyslexic pupils should highlight the key role of subject teachers and indicate appropriate strategies for supporting effective learning. There is evidence that what is good for the dyslexic learner is good for all learners – but subject teachers need to remain aware that although others can cope without this support, dyslexic pupils cannot (Peer 2001).

Support provision must be flexible to meet dyslexic pupils' changing needs, being tailored to a pupil's level of ability and learning style with relevant use of, for example, ICT. The National Curriculum Inclusion Statement (QCA/DfEE 1999) requires teachers to take action to respond to pupils' diverse needs by:

- creating effective learning environments;

- securing pupils' motivation and concentration;

- providing equality of opportunity through teaching approaches;

- setting targets for learning.

'Inclusion' often means that increasing demands are being made of teachers who find themselves in need of expertise in areas where they have no training (Peer 2001). Secondary subject teachers and school managers often feel ill-equipped to deal with the multiplicity of pupils' support needs in the mainstream curriculum. The National Union of Teachers survey (cited in *The Independent*, January 2007) reported that 77 per cent of teachers felt ill-equipped to deal with the problems of dyslexic pupils in their classrooms. The increasing number of dyslexia specialist teachers in schools may help to inform subject staff about dyslexia and enable then to analyse pupils' needs, devise effective support strategies and monitor the effectiveness of interventions (DfES 2001a: 75–6). However, there is a clear need to provide additional staff-development opportunities for all serving teachers and to introduce working with dyslexic pupils as a required element of pre-service teacher training.

Further reading

ELLIOT, D.L., DAVIDSON, J.K. AND LEWIN, J. (2007) *SCRE Research Report No 125: Literature Review of Current Approaches to the Provision of Education for Children with Dyslexia*, commissioned by HM Inspectorate of Education, The SCRE Centre, University of Glasgow, retrieved from www.scre.ac.uk/resreport/rr125/index.html.

MCKAY, N. (2004) 'The Case for Dyslexia Friendly Schools' in Reid, G. and Fawcett, A. (eds) *Dyslexia in Context: Research, Policy and Practice*, London: Whurr.

Cross-curricular issues

In this chapter, readers will:

- become aware of the underpinning skills required to access the secondary curriculum;

- look at aspects of reading, writing, note-taking, discussion, memory, organisation and coordination that are likely to be affected by dyslexia;

- develop awareness of numeracy issues linked to the secondary subject curriculum;

- consider the adaptation of the secondary curriculum using a case study to set this in context.

Most secondary subject teachers assume that their students arrive from the primary school with the ability to read, write and compute. Even when dyslexic difficulties are identified as part of a student's learning profile, subject teachers may struggle to relate this to their subject. When told that a student is dyslexic, what subject teachers really want to know is *how* the dyslexia will affect learning in their particular subject. Specialist dyslexia teachers will provide subject colleagues with details about dyslexic students' strengths and weaknesses that can be used to inform the production of learning profiles and to predict barriers to learning that may give rise to the need for additional support provision, and this can be developed as the student begins to engage with the subject curriculum (Peer and Reid 2003: 60–2). Comments relating dyslexic students' underlying difficulties to barriers to learning in the curriculum and suggested strategies for minimising the effects of these may help subject teachers to anticipate the needs of dyslexic students and adjust their delivery of the curriculum appropriately (McKay 2005: 52–9).

Underpinning skills for the secondary curriculum

The skills required for students to access the secondary subject curriculum are:

- communication skills – reading, writing, listening, talking;

- memory skills – short-term (working) memory, sequencing;

- organisation and coordination – use of tools and equipment.
(Peer and Reid 2003: 9–12)

Dyslexic students will not necessarily experience difficulties in all of these categories, and some will demonstrate strengths in areas where other students may struggle. The profiles of dyslexic students should identify both possible strengths and probable difficulties, according to the demands of each subject in the curriculum (Dodds and Thomson 1999).

Communication

Most teachers expect dyslexic students to have difficulties with reading and writing – but not all will experience the same problems, and many will have already developed strategies compensating for any weaknesses. Reading in the subject curriculum has a number of different functions, and dyslexic students may cope well with some of these but struggle with others (Cogan and Flecker 2004: 2–3).

Reading for information

Even dyslexic students who can read with a high level of comprehension are likely to read and process text much more slowly than teachers might expect (Shaywitz 2003: 52–4). Many have to read text several times to make sense of content, and are unable to pick up from where they left off if interrupted, slowing their reading rate even more. Teachers can help by ensuring that all text materials are clearly legible and by allowing dyslexic students to scan text to a computer with text-to-speech software. When planning lessons teachers might use video or audio recordings to support/illustrate content and create opportunities for student discussion of topics.

Additional support strategies

- Allow extra time;

- highlight key words/information;

- number lines and paragraphs – give page references;

- issue reading ruler/tinted overlay;

- provide electronic dictionaries, specialised software, and so on.

Teachers should ensure that print is not the only source of subject information for students – though recording or scanning materials is often less simple than it appears and copyright issues must be considered.

Reading aloud

Even those dyslexic students who are making good progress with reading may panic if asked to read in public and progress might be jeopardised by the experience. They may unintentionally change or obscure meaning and are very sensitive to being corrected publicly, adversely affecting self-esteem. For many, even the thought of reading aloud in class, in front of peers is a nightmare (Houston 2002: 28). Sometimes they experience visual distortions, especially when stressed, making it difficult to focus on text, causing embarrassment or frustration resulting in distress or inappropriate behaviour.

Teachers should accept dyslexic students as volunteer readers if they become aware they have prepared a section of text. If reading aloud is an essential part of a lesson, they should be given their segment in advance to allow them to rehearse and resolve any possible difficulties – teachers might arrange a signal to alert dyslexic students when they will be called on to read, allowing time to get ready.

Additional support strategies

- Enlarge font, increase line spacing;

- *never* ask a student with dyslexia to read aloud *without advance warning*;

- ensure that key subject information is read aloud only by a competent reader.

Dyslexic students who have auditory–verbal difficulties may be unable to process information that is read aloud, so it is important to provide visual support that will help them to understand content – e.g. a picture or diagram related to the text used as an attention focus.

Close reading

In many subjects, understanding is tested or reinforced by reading activities – a text passage followed by questions, multiple-choice exercises or filling blanks using key words (cloze). In exercises such as these, students' reading ability may determine success rather than knowledge or understanding of the subject. Dyslexic students may have additional difficulties with multiple-choice questions due the similarity of the choices offered; they may be unable to recognise key words out of context. They may also struggle to locate key information in text passages, have to re-read to understand content and be unable to relate the questions to the text.

Subject teachers should bear in mind that it takes dyslexic students longer to read the questions, compose answers in their heads, then get them down on paper, and that entitlement to support extends to assessments. Providing access arrangements for tests requiring fluent reading skills, such as student/teacher discussion, practical tasks, and interpretation of diagrams or illustrations of subject content might raise the attainment of all students (Johnston in Reid and Fawcett 2004: 253).

Additional support strategies

● Arrange extra time for dyslexic students to complete tests;

● provide the same level of reading support for tests as given in class;

● provide a list of vocabulary required and ICT use to complete cloze exercises;

● present information in charts or diagrams and illustrate text;

● conduct a class revision session before any test;

● provide a study guide explaining key terms and concepts.

Dyslexic students should be given the same level of support for assessments that is normally provided in the subject classroom (SQA 2004: 6).

Handwriting

Many students with dyslexia have poor fine motor skills and handwriting is slow, laboured and non-automatic, lacking fluency. They may be unable to write continuously without frequent rests. Not only is written work illegible but there may be unusual spatial organisation of the page with words widely spaced or tightly squashed together with margins ignored and writing off the line. Diagrams may be incorrectly labelled, wrongly proportioned or reversed and columns misaligned (McKay 2005: 198–202). Messy written work may result in a reader assuming carelessness and content that matches presentation – which is not necessarily the case for many dyslexic students who have done the best they can. When marking dyslexic students' work teachers should not penalise for poor presentation of work or bizarre spelling (Reid and Green 2007: 97).

Additional support strategies

- Allow extra time for extended writing;

- encourage alternatives to writing, e.g. recordings, ICT, dictation;

- allow students to rest/shake out their hands;

- issue model answers and spelling prompts;

- provide blank copies of diagrams/charts/tables for completion.

Subject teachers are not expected to teach dyslexic students handwriting, but, where graphic skills are part of the subject curriculum, they should offer strategies for improving these.

Extended writing

Dyslexic students often avoid writing, finding it stressful and exhausting; written work may take a long time and be illegible, full of spelling errors, with little punctuation and poor organisation. Dyslexic students are acutely aware of their difficulties, often feeling frustrated by their inability to express their understanding through writing. This makes it difficult for them to demonstrate their grasp of a subject to the same extent as other students. There may be a huge difference between their ability to tell you something and their ability to write it down (Cogan and Flecker 2004: 180–1). They struggle to plan/organise writing, unable to write in logical sequence, often not answering questions set, and are unable to use appropriate subject terminology. Most cannot proofread or identify errors in own writing.

Subject teachers should issue writing guidelines and paragraph headings to support the structure of extended writing and not penalise dyslexic students for poor presentation of work or bizarre spelling, marking only on the content of an assignment. Alternatives to extended writing should be accepted, e.g. charts/diagrams, mind maps, using bullet points or recording voice files to be transcribed later.

Additional support strategies

- Allow rests and build-in 'thinking' time;

- provide ICT and teach keyboarding and editing skills;

- encourage dictation to expand content;

- provide templates and model required responses;

- list key words and terms;

- highlight errors and suggest corrections/amendments.

The writing difficulties of many dyslexic students are often resolved by the introduction of ICT (Thomson in Reid and Fawcett 2004: 312) – and subject teachers should make an effort to ensure that this is readily accessible in the classroom.

Note-taking: teacher talk

Dyslexic students frequently have great difficulty taking notes from teachers' talk (Cogan and Flecker 2004: 117). Phonological processing difficulties cause them to lag behind and rushing to catch up invariably results in missing sections and illegible writing that even they cannot read or understand after an interval – even a very short one. They may be unable to process what the teacher is saying quickly enough to make sense and cannot listen and write at the same time. They may also have great difficulty taking personal notes from text, video, audio or ICT sources.

Note-taking: copying

For students who have dyslexia – especially those with visual processing and short-term memory difficulties – copying may be impossible. The results will certainly be unreliable and inaccurate (Reid and Green 2007: 94). When copying, a dyslexic student looks up, visually 'grabs' a little information, writes it down then repeats the process over and over, rarely demonstrating any comprehension of the material (Thomson and Chinn in Fawcett 2001: 287).

To ensure that dyslexic students have accurate subject notes, teachers could issue copies or identify a 'partner' whose notes can be photocopied as soon as possible after a lesson (perhaps by a TA).

Additional support strategies

- Allow a scribe or recorder (digital or tape);

- issue vocabulary prompts in advance;

- write any technical words on the board;

- teach use of bullet points/abbreviations/summaries/mind maps/diagrams;

- provide a framework for note taking;

- provide lesson summaries.

Unsupported copying should *never* be the *only* source of subject information.

Listening and talking

Some dyslexic students misuse familiar words and have difficulty remembering new or unfamiliar words – resulting in reluctance to talk in class. They often struggle to respond appropriately to questions due to the need to process the language first before being able to process the question. If a teacher speaks quickly, or gives too much information at once, dyslexic students will probably catch only parts of this (Reid and Green 2007: 4) and may be reluctant to admit that they missed information, preferring the teacher and classmates to believe that they were not paying attention. Dyslexic students may be slow to respond to a teacher's spoken instructions and find that the rest of the class is getting on with a piece of work while they have no idea where to begin, often asking for a page number immediately after the teacher has given it. They may misunderstand complicated questions, confuse sequences of instructions or fail to respond to questions even when they know the answer.

Additional support strategies

- Summarise teacher discourse;

- provide a relevant attention focus for listening;

- repeat instructions throughout a lesson;

- encourage the use of physical prompts – e.g. listing items using fingers;

- allow 'thinking' time to process input and construct responses.

Discussion

Some course requirements require the promotion of discussion within the classroom (Dargie in Peer and Reid 2001: 74–5) but dyslexic students may be unable to remember questions/instructions under discussion or be slow in processing language to respond to others' comments in good time resulting in them contributing apparently irrelevant remarks or contributions. Short-term memory problems may add to problems with turn-taking and dyslexic students may interrupt others to comment, afraid they will forget what they wanted to say if they don't speak at once.

Many subject teachers encourage students to 'brainstorm' or work together in groups to solve problems or to plan and complete course work – many dyslexic students excel at this, but some find it an additional challenge.

Additional support strategies

- Provide a structure for discussion with spaces for notes;

- encourage the use of turn-taking strategies;

- arrange cues to allow comments and ask if there are more before closing;

- ensure all students are aware of dyslexics' slow processing and wait for them to contribute.

Short-term (working) memory

The structure of the secondary curriculum offers additional challenges that may put considerable pressure on dyslexic students who have problems with their short-term memory. Some cannot hold as much information in working memory as other students (Kay and Yeo 2003: 14) finding it hard to remember instructions just after they were given or carry out all the steps in problem solving. Some dyslexic students are unable to hold numbers in short-term memory while doing calculations or forget what they were going to say in the middle of a sentence or while waiting for a pause in the conversation. Difficulties accessing long-term memory reduce working-memory capacity and slow the ability to recall familiar sequences or to select and apply previously learned procedures to current activities.

Teachers should bear in mind that all students remember bizarre or amusing incidents more easily and incorporate these into subject delivery to teach key concepts.

Additional support strategies

- Give one instruction at a time;

- allow extra time for problem solving;

- encourage the use of notebooks, reference cards and checklists;

- teach mnemonics and rhymes to aid memory;

- permit personal prompts, e.g. markers, notebooks, PDA;

- allow the use of calculators, provide ICT solutions, teach 'working' notes.

Dyslexic students tend to lose themselves (and their possessions) regularly and they may be unable to retrace their steps because they have no memory of how they arrived at a place.

Visual memory

Although it is not the role of subject teachers to check that student's eyes have been tested to identify any visual impairment, they could request this if visual skills are in doubt – though teenagers often refuse to wear glasses, preferring to fail at reading than face possible ridicule by classmates. Dyslexic students may cheerfully accept poor vision as a reason for difficulties experienced in the subject curriculum.

Those who experience visual-processing difficulties may complain of visual distortions/words moving around when reading, headaches, dizziness or nausea; they may rub their eyes, blink rapidly when concentrating; complain of scratchy or itchy eyes when using a computer. They may also complain they can't see the board, that the page or room is too bright and hurts their eyes.

Although conditions related to visual deficits can be helped by introducing tinted overlays or lenses (Jordan 2000: 20–2) teachers can also help by adjusting classroom lighting and adopting teaching styles that support weak visual processing (Irlen 1991: 176–8).

Additional support strategies

- Enlarge print or change font and line spacing;

- provide audio versions of longer texts;

- seat students near the board, out of direct sunlight away from fluorescent lights;

- scan worksheets to a computer, adjust size and use text–speech software;

- adjust monitor colour and brightness/contrast settings or use a screen filter.

Organisation and coordination

Memory and perception seem to play a large part in personal organisation so it is not surprising that many dyslexic students have difficulties in this area – they may forget essential books, equipment and homework or which day of the week it is, and follow the wrong timetable or get lost, being unable to find the way around when corridors all look the same. Organising life around a timetable (Fawcett in Peer and Reid 2001: 270) and remembering which books to take to school on any given day can be very difficult for dyslexic students whose coping strategies vary from taking no books at all to carrying all books all the time. They are often late to arrive at school and at subject classrooms, forget homework or hand it in late and may take a very long time settling to tasks.

Many dyslexic students spend a disproportionate amount of time searching for books and equipment, often forgetting what they are looking for.

They may have problems in corridors/stairs being unable to anticipate others' actions and some are unable to judge distance/speed or play team and ball games.

Additional support strategies

- Provide personal checklists for books/equipment;
- work with parents and colleagues to develop timekeeping;
- ask parents to monitor homework;
- use various timetable formats – e.g. different days in different colours;
- release early from class, or retain till crowds disperse;
- remain aware of fine motor problems when planning classroom activities;
- arrange extra practice for practical activities and sports.

Persistent fine and gross motor difficulties have been linked to dyslexia for many years (Peer and Reid 2003: 10–11) and dyslexic students often appear clumsy and uncoordinated, due to deficits in perceptual skills and speed of visual and auditory information processing. Provision of structured activities to develop these difficulties will lead to improved learning outcomes (Portwood 2003: 99).

Strategies to help dyslexic students determine their own position in relation to others and to anticipate common hazards – such as doors opening towards them, passing people on stairs – must be specifically taught, as they lack the 'automatic' ability to identify and predict common hazards in the environment. Subject teachers should consider teaching laboratory/workshop safety in a multi-sensory way in order to ensure that dyslexic students use all of their senses to decide when it is safe to carry out practical work.

Practical activities

Practical tasks such as measuring, cutting out or reading scales could be a source of difficulty for dyslexic students in subject classes (Peer and Reid 2003: 10–11). Some may have motor-planning problems affecting the ability to predict or follow a series of steps in the right order; other have fine/gross motor problems affecting ability to manipulate objects and write, affecting the completion of practical tasks – they may have a strange/awkward way of holding tools and equipment, lack the fine motor skills required to draw/measure accurately and be unable to use a ruler to draw straight lines. They often have little or no understanding of scale, experience confusion about appropriate measures for different tasks and are unable to complete practical activities involving direction.

Additional support strategies

- Provide tools and instruments with handling aids;

- issue isometric paper for drawing activities and provide transparent rulers;

- provide roller/sticky rulers for accurate measuring;

- issue a sample page layout, clearly showing location for working;

- use flow charts for reference, showing sequence of steps;

- introduce visual cues such as arrows to indicate directions.

Dyslexic students' inability to record results of experiments clearly and logically and to construct suitable tables for recording data may be easily resolved by teachers issuing skeleton notes for completion.

Underpinning numeracy issues

Understanding mathematical language is a problem for many dyslexic students – even those who are gifted mathematicians may struggle with reading and spelling specialist vocabulary (DfES 2001c: 2). Maths teachers who emphasise the mechanics of number work at the expense of teaching the meaning of the subject language could use images or examples from a real context to address this. Some dyslexic students know how to do every step in a calculation, but get the steps out of sequence, ending up with the wrong answer, whereas others are able to produce correct answers but are unable to show the working to explain the process.

Often their speed of processing numbers is very slow compared to others and they forget what they are doing, losing track mid-process. They may lack understanding of place value and misalign columns of figures – doing this left to right, start calculations from the left, subtract top from bottom or carry a number the wrong way. Dyslexic students may be unable to estimate or give approximate answers.

Additional support strategies

- Make addition/multiplication grids and ready-reckoners available;

- issue squared paper to help with organisation and accuracy;

- use concrete materials when possible;

- allow calculator/number square use to help the speed of processing;

- encourage students to note what they are doing to prevent them losing track mid process;

- issue worksheets with numbers already entered.

Teachers should bear in mind that many dyslexic students are inconsistent workers, managing to do something correctly one day, but unable to repeat it the next.

Shape/symbol confusion

Some dyslexic students may struggle to distinguish between different symbols – e.g. confusing + with × in number work – and there may be particular difficulties when writing indices – positioning these inappropriately. Identification of shapes and symbols and the placement of different symbols is an important element of several subjects in the secondary curriculum; dyslexic students may also confuse subject language referring to symbols and shapes or be unable to sequence formulae notation correctly (McKay 2005: 203–5).

Additional support strategies

● Display shape/symbols charts in the classroom;

● issue reference cards showing essential subject symbols/shapes/formulae;

● use templates that emphasise the different qualities of shapes;

● use colour to code lines and symbols and identify aspects of shapes.

Although some students with dyslexia may have problems identifying simple shapes, the three-dimensional visualisation skills of other dyslexics help them to 'see' relationships and concepts more quickly and clearly than others.

Directionality and time

Dyslexic difficulties linked to orientation and direction may affect the understanding of patterns and sequences as well as making it difficult for students to cope with aspects of some subjects, e.g. geography, chemistry. Pupils may have little or no sense of direction confusing left and right and may also have problems reading figures in the correct direction/order or have difficulty with the vocabulary of directionality and position – above/below, forward/back. Dyslexic students may have difficulty extracting information from tables, charts and graphs or be unable to tell the time on an analogue clock (DfES 2001c: 9). When asked what time it is, they may say something ridiculous like 'It's half past quarter to' and have difficulty estimating the passage of time, being unable to work out when 'in 15 minutes' would be.

Additional support strategies

- Use arrows and movement to help to show directions/positions;

- set numbered steps to be checked off as they are done;

- use L-shaped card to read from tables; transparent ruler to read charts/graphs; colour-code axes;

- use a countdown digital clock or hands of a 'round' clock to show time actually passing.

Adapting the secondary curriculum

A small number of dyslexic students will experience severe difficulties in the secondary subject curriculum due to failure to master the early stages of literacy and numeracy, and the school's specialist staff should advise colleagues how to support these students' access to the curriculum (DfES 2001a: 71). Cross-curricular support is vital as students are taught by several teachers, and not all will provide the same level of support for accessing the curriculum. What often works is a combination of specifically tailored support in combination with appropriately differentiated teaching across the curriculum so that dyslexic students can access the subject curriculum. The Secondary Curriculum Review (QCA 2007a) describes 'Waves' of support for students who have been identified for School Action or School Action Plus interventions (DfES 2001a: 68–72). Wave 2 provision – to help students apply their learning in mainstream lessons – is a tight, structured programme of small-group support in addition to whole-class lessons as part of a differentiated approach. Successful Wave 2 intervention gets students back on track to meet national expectations.

The aim of Wave 3 teaching is to maximise progress and to minimise performance gaps by providing one-to-one or very small group support delivered by a specialist teacher or highly trained teaching assistant to support students towards the achievement of very specific targets. Dyslexic students who are still in the early stages of literacy/numeracy acquisition will probably need this tuition and time has to be 'created' within an already crowded curriculum to ensure that this is possible. The case studies in the DfES (2006) Secondary National Strategy pilot programme – *Intensifying Support* – describe literacy progress units where students were extracted for intensive tuition, and where time was found by using either non-class time – before or after school – or morning registration/tutor time. However, not all schools are able to offer such blocks of time – some may have a shorter registration period, others may have activities already in place. The case studies (DfES 2006) illustrate other options. Extracting 'target' students from parts of several subject lessons for specialist tuition proved unpopular with subject teachers and resulted in students losing ground in the subject curriculum, though making progress with literacy.

An option used in many schools is to reduce the number of secondary subjects for a severely dyslexic student. There is an assumption that if dyslexic students have not yet mastered the reading and grammar of English and experience severe phonological processing difficulties, they will be unable to learn a modern foreign language, and many schools apply to remove them from this subject. But this assumption is not always true (Crombie and McColl in Peer and Reid 2001: 54–6).

Case study: Adam, age 12 – adapted curriculum

Adam was identified as dyslexic at primary school when he failed to make progress with reading. He was given daily reading lessons at primary and slowly began to make progress, but his reading was still very poor when he transferred to secondary school and his spelling/writing skills were virtually non-existent. It was agreed with parents at transition meetings that his daily reading sessions would continue and he would follow a structured writing/spelling programme including the introduction of ICT. However, there was no discussion of how the time needed for this programme would be found.

After a few weeks, Adam arrived home despondent and told his mother that he did not get to go to Art – he had to go for extra reading. When she contacted the school, she found that this was indeed the case. She protested

– 'But he is very good at Art.'

And the support teacher agreed, 'That's why we took him out.'

Mother protested again, 'But he really enjoys Art.'

The support teacher again agreed, 'Yes, but he needs to learn to read.'

Mother tried again, 'Is there no other subject he could come out of?'

'Yes,' replied the support teacher, 'he's also very good at Craft & Design, so we are taking him out of that too next week to work on his spelling.'

Adam refused to attend the tutorials and persistently turned up at his subject classes. After several meetings and with the full support of his Art and Craft & Design teachers, Adam was returned to the subjects where he was doing well and a tailored curriculum was agreed. His daily reading programme was rearranged to take place before school started. He was extracted from some Geography and English lessons – agreed with the teachers – for tuition in writing and spelling. He was much happier and started to make progress in literacy skills. He consistently achieved in the top 5 per cent of the Art and Craft & Design classes.

Different schools take different approaches to the adaptation of the secondary curriculum so that students who require specialist tuition have time for this – but it is important that the wishes of parents and students are taken into account when proposals are made about changing the curriculum to create time for extra reading or maths lessons (DfES 2001b: 21, 27–8).

Further reading

HENDERSON, A. (1998) *Maths for the Dyslexic: A Practical Guide*, London: David Fulton.

REID, G. AND GREEN, S. (2007) *100 Ideas for Supporting Pupils with Dyslexia*, London: Continuum.

CHAPTER 6

Subject teachers' guides

In this chapter, readers will:

- become aware of the developmental nature of dyslexia;

- look at dyslexia in the context of the secondary curriculum;

- consider the need to take account of the impact of dyslexia when planning lessons and setting homework;

- develop awareness of the need to assess the readability level of curriculum materials;

- understand that a teacher's writing style and presentation of curriculum materials will affect dyslexic students' access to these;

- explore subject-specific barriers to learning and consider strategies to minimise these.

Because dyslexia is developmental in nature, some students who coped with the early stages of literacy acquisition may experience difficulties with higher order skills that do not appear until the secondary stage so it is important that subject teachers are aware that they may be the first to note signs of dyslexia in some students. Often, a discrepancy between a student's subject ability and the quality (and quantity) of written work, for no apparent reason, is observed and this should be referred to the school's specialist staff for investigation (Thomson 2007c: 8).

Dyslexia in context

It is important that secondary teachers consider dyslexia in the context of their own subject, remembering that:

- dyslexia can be mild to severe and occur at any ability level;

- dyslexic students often experience difficulties in education, some of them hidden;

- dyslexic students often have natural talents and creative abilities.

(Peer in Peer and Reid 2001: 3)

Learning differences related to dyslexia may cause unexpected difficulties within the subject curriculum, so students may appear disaffected; they may persistently underachieve, concealing difficulties – causing poor progress to be attributed to lack of interest or effort, misbehaviour or illness (Thomson 2006: 17). This makes it difficult for teachers to detect dyslexia in the context of the subject curriculum and may result in a delay in action to reduce barriers to learning in the delivery of the curriculum.

Lesson planning

Subject teachers should anticipate the possible learning needs of dyslexic students when preparing lesson materials (see **Photocopiable 6.1** on pp. 139–40). In addition to reading and writing difficulties, they may experience problems with auditory and/or visual processing resulting in:

- short-term (working) memory difficulties;

- lack of reading/writing speed and fluency;

- weak organisational skills;

- directional confusion;

- poor physical coordination and lack of automaticity.

(Reid 2004: 14–15)

Teachers should avoid approaches that require unnecessary dependence on text; provide scaffolding support to guide the flow of work; and allow extra time for dyslexic students to organise thoughts and develop new skills (McKay 2005: 58–9).

Homework tasks should be planned as part of the lesson – dyslexic students have problems with time management and prioritising, resulting in incomplete and poorly presented work, so teachers should anticipate problems with this (Reid and Green 2007: 68).

Selecting reading materials

When selecting reading materials, subject teachers should consider that most dyslexic readers have to concentrate harder than their classmates and will take more time to make sense of texts, often having to re-read in order to process content.

Dyslexic readers may experience visual discomfort, often losing their place. Some may experience visual overload (Jordan 2000: 20) and distortions of the text itself ranging from poor print resolution to moving text (Irlen 1991: 29–51) and this can result in lack of concentration, fatigue and headaches. Some materials can make these problems worse, so teachers should try to avoid shiny whiteboards and glossy white paper. The number of words on a page and the size, spacing and font of text may increase reading difficulties, so teachers should anticipate these and provide supports – e.g. tinted overlays – or copy/enlarge text on a coloured background. Increasingly, textbooks are produced on non-glare paper and large print versions are often available, so teachers can arrange for these to be provided – though the readability level should be checked (Cogan and Flecker 2004: 25–8).

Readability

This can be checked when using Microsoft Word – on the menu bar, click Tools, Options, Spelling, and Grammar then tick the Readability request. Readability scores are based on the average number of syllables per word and words per sentence.

- **Flesch Reading Ease score** – rates text on a 100-point scale; the higher the score, the easier it is to understand the document.

- **Flesch–Kincaid Grade Level score** – rates text on a US grade-school level – e.g. a score of 5.0 means that a 10-year-old, can understand the document.

Teachers should change high readability scores by using shorter sentences, not by removing important subject terminology.

Subject teachers are not expected to be able to deliver the curriculum without setting reading tasks, so they should consider providing additional support for dyslexic students for these.

Preparation of curriculum materials

Dyslexic students process information and may read differently from classmates, but subject teachers can make curricular materials more easily accessible by making simple changes to the way information and activities are presented (BDA 2006b).

Teacher's writing style

If a teacher's normal style is to use long, complicated sentences, dyslexic students will struggle to understand. All students will benefit if teachers write in short simple sentences, number lines and paragraphs, highlight key words/ new subject vocabulary and distinguish between instructions and explanations.

Presentation of materials

If materials look attractive, students' interest will be caught quickly and if illustrations and diagrams break up text, dyslexic students may be able to determine what is required without having to ask for help to get started. Using italics or underlining can make words appear to run together and creates additional problems for dyslexic readers. Key information should be highlighted and separated from the rest of the text – e.g. in a box – and continuous prose broken up using bullets or numbers.

Subject-specific strengths, difficulties and support strategies

The underpinning literacy difficulties of many dyslexic students will impact on their learning across the curriculum and those who also experience difficulties in maths may be further disadvantaged due to the need to apply calculation, measurement and direction in practical activities. Self-esteem issues may also have a powerful impact on dyslexic students' ability to cope with the demands of the subject curriculum (Hales in Peer and Reid 2001: 232–3) and teachers may find that reference to the success of well-known dyslexic people will improve dyslexic students' confidence (see www.xtraordinarypeople.com/).

English

The difficulties in communication experienced by dyslexic students across the secondary curriculum are more obvious, creating more difficulties in the English classroom. Not all dyslexic students experience the same pattern of difficulties, so grouping several in the same class could increase a teacher's workload rather than making it easier to respond to their needs. Teachers of English may face the additional challenge of working with bilingual dyslexic students, whose needs are even more complex (Deponio *et al.* in Peer and Reid 2000: 59). Self-esteem issues may impact on dyslexic students' performance and behaviour in the English classroom since this is where their difficulties are most apparent.

Significant strengths of dyslexic students

- Excellent oral skills;
- vivid imaginations;
- originality and creativity in writing.

Additional barriers to learning

- Tire quickly when reading/writing and quality of work deteriorates;
- give up when faced with long texts and small print;
- confuse the names of characters in a text;
- struggle to use the correct vocabulary to comment on texts.

Additional support strategies

- For talks, encourage the use of simple prompt cards stapled together in order;
- issue essay guidelines and paragraph headings to support the structure of writing;
- provide models of different types of expressive/transactional writing;
- issue summaries of texts;
- provide alternatives to text sources, e.g. audio books.

The difficulties dyslexic students experience in the English classroom are examined in detail by Pughe and Turner (2004).

Dyslexia and Maths

Although dyslexic students are often better at coping with numbers than reading, this is not always so. Underpinning difficulties with numeracy (see Chapter 5) will affect how they learn in the Maths class.

Significant strengths of dyslexic students

- Strongly developed spatial awareness;
- intuitive ability to manipulate data;
- ability to understand complex relationships instantly.

Reading and Maths

Numbers are rarely met in isolation from text and reading difficulties may mask mathematical ability. The language of mathematics is difficult to decode – e.g. vertices, isosceles – and rarely gives contextual clues to help with meaning. The flow of reading in Maths may not always be from left to right, as it often includes tables and diagrams that many dyslexic students find confusing (McKay 2005: 157).

Additional barriers to learning

- Misreading changes the meaning of questions;

- reading from left to right results in diagrams/tables not being identified as part of a question;

- difficulty understanding positional/directional vocabulary, e.g. above, beside;

- difficulty understanding abbreviations.

Additional support strategies

- Teach mathematical language as 'foreign' vocabulary, explaining meaning in context;

- check language as well as number processes in Maths exercises;

- highlight any tables/charts/diagrams as part of a question;

- issue abbreviations decoding prompts.

Memory and Maths

Some students have memory-related problems, which can create difficulties in relation to retaining number facts and tables, number order, sequencing and place value. Memorising mathematical facts is challenging for many dyslexic students and difficulties in directionality and sequencing can make some tasks so difficult that even those who are very good at Maths may be unable to cope (Henderson *et al.* 2003: 127).

Additional barriers to learning

- Cannot memorise multiplication tables;

- unable to hold numbers in their heads while carrying out calculations;

- cannot copy numbers accurately from one place to another;

- inability to show working – they 'see' Maths in their head, but can't explain.

Additional support strategies

- Aid recall using gimmicks such as finger tables, rhythm and rhyme;

- develop a sequence checklist for calculation procedures;

- issue exemplars that clearly indicate required layout;

- teach formulae in a 'fun' way using mnemonics, colour coding and jingles.

For additional information, Maths teachers might consult Anne Henderson's *Maths for the Dyslexic: A Practical Guide* (1998), and Kay and Yeo's *Dyslexia and Maths* (2003).

Dyslexia and Information and Communications Technology

ICT use can increase dyslexic students' independence. Some dyslexics have great difficulty moving information from short-term to long-term memory – leading to low self-esteem and a failure to engage with some aspects of the curriculum. Using ICT can boost students' self-confidence and encourage them to develop strategies to compensate for their difficulties (Crivelli in Peer and Reid 2001: 218). ICT can enhance access to the secondary curriculum, providing support in class without frequent requests for additional teacher intervention.

Significant strengths of dyslexic students

- Multi-sensory learning styles;

- multi-dimensional thinking and perception;

- intuitive ability to manipulate data;

- a high level of curiosity, originality and creativity.

Computing and Business Studies

Dyslexic students lack automaticity in reading and writing tasks but the impact of this is often less when ICT is used – they are more likely to produce acceptable course work using ICT – and they may be less fatigued than if required to write by hand. Some dyslexic students recognise computer operations – input–processing–output – as similar to the way their own minds work.

Spelling difficulties of many dyslexic students will lead to particular problems, especially when searching for information. Sequencing problems can be minimised by the use of editing features in a word processing package, or supported by the introduction of additional software.

Additional barriers to learning

- Difficulty recognising correct spelling from spellchecker lists;

- inability to operate a keyboard and listen to the teacher at the same time;

- confuses ICT vocabulary with the same words used in different contexts;

- visual distortions experienced on the monitor.

Additional support strategies

- Encourage Google use (recognises wrong spelling and offers corrections);

- explain/illustrate specialist meanings of ICT terminology;

- adjust colour, brightness and font settings to minimise visual discomfort;

- provide screen filters to reduce glare and flickering.

For additional information, ICT teachers might consult 'Using ICT to Help Dyslexic Children and Adults' by Crivelli *et al.* in Reid and Fawcett (2004) and many will enjoy Thomas West's *In the Mind's Eye* (1997).

Science subjects

The possible strengths of dyslexic students and barriers to their attainment should be considered in the context of individual science subjects, although there are some common elements that all science teachers should consider when constructing programmes of work. Those dyslexic students who experience difficulties in Maths will be further disadvantaged due to the need to apply certain mathematical skills in sciences, particularly Physics (Holmes in Peer and Reid 2001: 92).

Strengths of dyslexic students in the sciences

- Lateral thinking – a unique approach to problem solving;

- ability to design interesting experiments;

- asking insightful questions.

Theory and preparation

Additional barriers to learning

- Inability to process information in tables, charts or graphs;

- does not label diagrams accurately;

- problems writing scientific formulae;

- confusion of scientific terminology with other uses – e.g. 'conductor';

- difficulty understanding and remembering scientific symbols.

Additional support strategies

- Explain how to interpret tables/diagrams in context;

- provide blank tables, charts, and so on already labelled;

- use illustrations to help recall of scientific terminology;

- enlarge formulae to make use of upper/lower case, sub/superscript clear – use ICT and a formula prompt sheet.

Practical activities

Additional barriers to learning

- Difficulty locating, selecting and using appropriate equipment;
- struggle to read scales and measurements;
- confuse similarly named equipment and substances;
- difficulty recording data when carrying out a practical task.

Additional support strategies

- Label equipment cupboards with pictures;
- show and name equipment when giving instructions;
- encourage students to check each others' equipment for safety points;
- set up workstations in advance;
- use prompts and arrows to indicate directions and help reading scales;
- allow dictation of results during an experiment.

For additional information, Physics teachers might consult 'Dyslexia and Physics' by P. Holmes and Biology teachers refer to 'Dyslexia and Biology' by C.A. Howlett, both in Peer and Reid (2001).

Home Economics

This subject offers all students the opportunity to acquire essential life skills as well as a range of vocational experiences. Practical demonstrations and opportunities to work with peers allow dyslexic students to experience success on a regular basis – something that is not often possible in the secondary curriculum (Hales in Peer and Reid 2001: 240). Difficulties may arise due to motor planning and fine-control problems that may make the acquisition of some skills slow, and dyslexic students' short-term memory problems may cause them to appear disorganised and confused. Dyslexic students should be given support for essential planning, recording and evaluating of practical activities.

Significant strengths of dyslexic students

- Multi-sensory learning styles;
- an acute awareness of the environment;
- original and creative approaches to problem solving.

Additional barriers to learning

- Disorganised and messy work stations;

- inability to carry out an activity while listening;

- confusion of subject vocabulary with the same words in different contexts;

- failure to collect all ingredients/utensils before starting to prepare food;

- forgetting whether ingredients have been added.

Additional support strategies

- Introduce colour-coding to help maintain tidy work stations;

- construct personal flip charts for recipes giving one instruction per page;

- use visual clues to illustrate 'technical' instructions such as 'beat';

- issue checklists of ingredients/equipment for students to tick.

Home Economics teachers and students might enjoy dyslexic Jamie Oliver's book *The Naked Chef* (1999).

Art, Craft & Design

These subjects provide many dyslexic students with an opportunity to excel, since many have visual strengths. Dyslexic differences that make reading, writing, and spelling difficult are often linked to high ability where perception is important and individual interpretation is required (West 1997: 12).

Significant strengths of dyslexic students

- Strongly developed spatial awareness;

- multi-dimensional thinking and perception.

Additional barriers to learning

- Failure to develop automaticity of equipment use;

- difficulty organising work space;

- may sacrifice originality and creativity to complete a task;

- weaknesses in some graphic skills.

Additional support strategies

- Demonstrate skills and techniques;

- design flow charts showing the sequences of steps in activities;

- keep tasks open-ended, do not specify outcomes;

- encourage students to try different approaches/interpretations;

- break-down graphic tasks into small steps;

- encourage ICT use for graphic design and writing.

Fran Renaldi's book *Dyslexia and Design & Technology* (2003) will be of interest to teachers of design as will Thomas West's *In the Mind's Eye* (1997).

Music

Success in musical activity can boost a dyslexic student's self-esteem though dyslexia may adversely affect specific aspects of Music such as:

- interpreting musical notation;

- visual processing of written music;

- fingering and manual dexterity.

Limitations on working memory and lack of automaticity may be revealed when dyslexic students participate in musical activities. When playing instruments, they may appear to be reading musical notation when they have memorised the piece – and music reading errors may actually be due to faulty memory. A discrepancy between sight-reading and 'usual' performance is often an indication of a dyslexic difficulty affecting music (Ditchfield in Peer and Reid 2001: 151).

Significant strengths of dyslexic students

- Ability to 'hear' notes in their heads;

- ability to predict complex sounds from notation;

- high levels of creativity and originality.

Reading musical notation is very difficult for dyslexic learners and the impact of visual distortions can make it impossible. Terminology associated with tempo and style may be in another language that dyslexic musicians often struggle to interpret (Skeath 2007). Poor graphic skills may cause inaccurate written notation – the need to distribute notation across five lines leads to five times as many errors.

Additional barriers to learning

- Difficulties translating left–right notation into finger movements;

- musical notation may trigger visual distortions;

- two-handed playing and two-stave reading particularly difficult in piano playing;

- experience disorganisation when:
  - time signatures look like, but are not, fractions;
  - visual overload occurs while trying to process pages of music.

Additional support strategies

- The Music Publishers Association allows music to be photocopied for dyslexic musicians;

- use 'multi-sensory' methods to embed:
  - recall of fingerings;
  - recognition of rhythmic patterns;
  - the understanding of pitch.

- link colours to letter-names and use mnemonics to help remember facts;

- link musical language to common events – *diminuendo* linked to dimming lights;

- colour-code key signatures, and the positions of repeat marks;

- introduce singing to minimise reading difficulties;

- arrange peer support in groups/orchestra to keep the place.

Stress and the fear of failure can cause dyslexic musicians great anguish, but they can experience success provided they are given sufficient encouragement and understanding.

Instrumental teachers will find S. Oglethorpe's *Instrumental Music for Dyslexics: A Teaching Handbook* (2002) very useful, while all will be fascinated by the accounts of how some dyslexics can be highly gifted musicians in *Music and Dyslexia, Opening New Doors*, edited by Tim Miles and John Westcombe (2001).

Drama

Many dyslexics excel in performance arts and the successful may be excellent role models for those beginning to study Drama. Dyslexic students often have good improvisation skills but struggle to work from a script and the need to focus on the printed page may impair the ability to perform.

Significant strengths of dyslexic students

● Excellent oral skills, mimicry and timing;

● acute awareness of the environment;

● intrinsic ability to relate movement to speech;

● very observant, highly intuitive and perceptive;

● vivid imaginations, quirky and original.

Additional barriers to learning

● Continually lose the place/read the wrong lines in scripts;

● unable to cope with stage directions – they may already confuse left/ right;

● fail to remember what character they are representing.

Additional support strategies

● Issue large-print versions of scripts;

● highlight and use colour codes for individual parts;

● provide visual, auditory and tactile sources for improvisation;

● use large prompt cards for instructions, stage directions, and so on;

● issue costumes and props at an early stage to help students keep in character;

● encourage visual representation for developing story lines.

H. Eadon's book *Dyslexia and Drama* (2004) will help Drama teachers to enable dyslexic students to get the most from drama inside and outside the classroom. They may also be interested in Robin Gray's 'Drama: the Experience of Learning' in Peer and Reid (2001).

Physical Education (games, sports and outdoor activities)

Motor coordination difficulties may impact on dyslexic students' ability to participate effectively in some PE activities, especially ball games and team sports. They may struggle with some components of a PE course due to poor balance or be unable to judge speed and distance and may lack depth perception. However, many dyslexic students excel at individual sports such as athletics (Portwood 2003: 81) and others may succeed in small teams where there is little risk of collision with others.

Significant strengths of dyslexic students

- Acute awareness of the environment;

- ability to practice the same skill over and over;

- endurance and determination to succeed.

Additional barriers to learning

- Immature motor control and clumsiness, e.g. tripping over;

- difficulty putting a sequence of moves together smoothly;

- failure to develop automaticity in actions;

- poor hand–eye coordination causing problems in ball games;

- unable to listen and perform at the same time;

- misinterpretation of rules, trying to apply the rules for one game to another;

- inability to change direction when moving at speed.

Additional support strategies

- Introduce exercises to help develop motor control;

- use computer games/simulations to help develop sound/movement sequencing;

- arrange activities to develop binocular coordination using near and distant targets;

- demonstrate and model movements and techniques;

- combine verbal instructions with demonstrations;

- create wall displays in colour to show sports 'dos' and 'don'ts';

- use visual representations of tactics and strategies;

- issue pocket-size references that can be discreetly consulted.

Dyslexic students' experiences in other areas of the curriculum may have led to the development of a learning style underpinned by the determination to succeed at something, and the ability to practice for longer than others – often resulting in highly visible achievements in sporting performance.

PE and sports teachers will be interested in both Madeleine Portwood's book *Dyslexia and Physical Education* (2003) and *Head Strong: How to Get Physically and Mentally Fit* (2001) by Sir Steven Redgrave and Tony Buzan.

Social subjects (Classical Studies, Geography, History, Modern Studies, Philosophy, Religious Studies)

Social subjects require students to develop study and enquiry skills – to name, locate, select, organise, record, interpret, analyse and evaluate information and abstract ideas. The oral skills of discussion, debating and interviewing may be part of the development of enquiry skills and interacting with others. Although the underpinning literacy and numeracy difficulties of some dyslexic students may make the acquisition of these skills challenging, this does not mean that they will not excel in social subjects – those who have good visual processing skills may succeed in Geography whereas others with highly developed verbal processing abilities will do well in Philosophy, Classical and Modern Studies.

Dyslexic students may need extra time to respond to visual or auditory stimuli in order to think, question, deduce and form opinions and this will impact on their ability to participate in discussion. Since the need to plan, record and evaluate their classroom activities is essential, they should be offered a range of alternatives to writing, including ICT. Some aspects of Geography need underpinning Maths skills, so support strategies used by Maths teachers might be considered. Self-esteem issues affect performance and behaviour in the classroom and the cumulative effect of fatigue on performance should not be ignored.

Significant strengths of dyslexia students

- Multi-dimensional thinking and perception;

- curiosity, high awareness of the environment;

- a high level of empathy – intuitive and perceptive;

- original and creative approaches to problem solving.

Additional barriers to learning

- Difficulty using an index and other alphabetical references;

- difficulty extracting information from a pictorial source, map or chart;

- difficulty interpreting data presented in tables/graphs;

- inability to locate coordinates.

Additional support strategies

- Explain and illustrate terminology using visual examples;

- arrange access to electronic reference sources;

- issue only sections of maps to reduce problems locating coordinates;

- teach students to construct charts/timelines to sequence events;

- use picture sources arranged to show a sequence of events;

- issue pre-prepared blank tables, charts, and so on for completion;

- allow voice recorders for fieldwork and interviewing.

History teachers will find more information in *Dyslexia and History* (2005) by R. Dargie, and Geographers may be interested in 'Dyslexia and Geography' by F. Williams and J. Lewis in Peer and Reid (2001).

Modern Foreign Languages (MFL)

Learning a new language may not be easy for those dyslexic students who are struggling to acquire literacy in their first language (Crombie and McColl in Peer and Reid 2001: 55). Table 6.1 identifies additional challenges that dyslexic learners face when a new language is introduced and suggests some strategies that teachers might use to minimise these.

Modern Languages teachers can take advantage of dyslexic students' familiarity with strategies such as over-learning and multi-sensory practice to help them learn another language. Teachers may also find it helpful to apply what they know about how students learn a new language to help them understand the difficulties many dyslexic students experience with English – they must process the language first, in much the same way as students new to a foreign language translate back into English, before processing meaning (Schneider and Crombie 2003: 6–7).

Choice of language

MFL are not yet a compulsory part of the primary curriculum in England, but many schools have these on the timetable or as an extra-curricular activity. In Scotland, MFL are taught in all primary schools, and in Wales both English and Welsh are taught. Sometimes the language offered at secondary school depends on which language was available in the primary school – predominantly French in England and Scotland. Although French is the most common, it is the one that dyslexic students find most difficult because words are not written as they sound (BDA 2006c). German is much easier initially as it has common roots with English and words are spelt as they sound, but compound words and a formal grammar make it increasingly difficult. Italian is difficult at first as its sound system is quite different from English and there are many irregular verbs – but it does have a regular spelling system and it gets easier over time. The best language for dyslexic students to learn is one with a good sound–spelling relationship and a regular verb system with few irregularities – such as Spanish or even Japanese, where a different alphabet actually helps (University of Hull 2007).

More information may be found in 'Dyslexia and the teaching of Modern Foreign Languages' by M. Crombie and H. McColl in Peer and Reid (2001) and in *Dyslexia and Modern Foreign Languages: Gaining Success in an Inclusive Context* (2004) by M. Crombie and E. Schneider.

Table 6.1

Multi-sensory approaches to Modern Foreign Language learning

Challenges facing all foreign language learners	Additional barriers to learning for dyslexic learners	Multi-sensory strategies that can help all learners	Support strategies for dyslexic learners
VOCABULARY ACQUISITION: **Need to acquire large quantities of new language items in a relatively short time, to remember them for long periods of time, and to be able to recall them as required**	• Short-term and working memory difficulties • Auditory-verbal processing difficulties • Slow naming speed • Overload on working memory • Tendency to miss or reverse syllables • Word finding difficulty	• Use of vocabulary cards embodying text and pictures. These can be used selectively and repeatedly in game-like activities to support acquisition, to consolidate learning and to prompt recall • Class encouraged to compile a picture dictionary in book or poster form, using the same visuals	• Copies of vocabulary cards to be retained for additional practice and future revision • Similar vocabulary items can be incorporated into ICT software, e.g. Clicker Grids and used to enhance vocabulary card use • Frequent use of games like Snap and Matching Pairs to reinforce new vocabulary
SPEECH: **Need to learn how to pronounce and read aloud words that follow a different phonetic code.** **Need to learn how to say the words, to recognise them when they are spoken or read and to be able to write them reasonably accurately**	• Phonological awareness deficit/confusion • Effects of stress on accuracy of pronunciation and fluency • Difficulties re letter/sound relationships • Poor auditory discrimination • Links between reading and phonics weak or not understood • Visuo-perceptual difficulties • Orthographic difficulties • Mismatch between teaching and learning styles • Speed at which 'natural language' is spoken – mismatch with speed of processing information	• Vocabulary cards can be selected to illustrate and practice selected sound/text explanations • Teachers can use the same visual illustrations (on OHP/interactive white board) to support the introduction of textual forms of words • Vocabulary cards incorporate text, so that written and oral forms of the word can reinforce each other **Resources:** • Drake Language Master and cards http://websites.uk-plc.net/DRAKE_EDUCATIONAL_ASSOCIATES/ • Linguascope at www.linguascope.com • Textease at www.softease.com/products/studioct.htm	• Vocabulary cards can incorporate the same pictures, plus sound, and opportunities created to compare pupils' pronunciation with that of the teacher • Worksheets incorporating the same pictures can be used to set up writing activities • Use of ICT to reinforce reading • Use of Language Master to reinforce speaking and listening **Additional resources:** • Miniflashcard Language Games: MLG www.mlgpublishing.com/about • Clicker www.cricksoft.com/uk/: • BBC Primary French www.bbc.co.uk/schools/primaryfrench/parents/mfl_html.shtml

Table 6.1 (continued)

Multi-sensory approaches to Modern Foreign Language learning

Challenges facing all foreign language learners	Additional barriers to learning for dyslexic learners	Multi-sensory strategies that can help all learners	Support strategies for dyslexic learners
GRAMMAR: **Need to understand patterns of language, how words influence each other, how sentences are constructed, and how to construct sentences accurately**	• Sequencing difficulties • Difficulties with prediction in first language • Mismatch between learning and teaching styles • Failure to achieve automaticity and fluency affects language perception	• By adding language dice to sets of cards, grammatical associations can be explained visually, sentences can be manipulated, paradigms of possibilities set up • Games and activities provide practice	• Examples generated with cards and dice can be recorded in prepared grids and further examples found for homework and so on • Use of Linguascope website activities to extend experience of target language and reinforce vocabulary use
CONSOLIDATION AND PERFORMANCE: **Need for realistic settings with appropriate everyday useful language, e.g. phone conversations, and reading and listening practice. Teachers could encourage the use of the language in other subjects, target, e.g. Art staff might use French names of colours**	• Retention – the dyslexic learner needs more repetition and re-teaching in order to transfer data to long-term memory • Slow rate of language processing • Difficulties transferring learned skills • Coping with language at natural speed	• Over-learning through seeing, saying, hearing, writing and physical movement • Role play – acting out situations • Digital Language instruction – slow down speed of presentation initially	• Use of teacher developed/photocopiable resources to produce games that reinforce common language – e.g. Pelmanism – foods, clothes, prepositions, and so on • Video with subtitles in language being learned • Video, without subtitles, of familiar programmes in target language, e.g. Asterix cartoons • ICT – CD-ROM- based and on-line activities
CREATIVITY: **Need to generate language in new combinations; often 'personal language', but learners can not always think of things to say**	• Effects of fatigue and low self-esteem and the need to concentrate on practical difficulties may inhibit creative use of language • Problems with organisation and sequencing	• Picture cards can be selected to act as 'prompts' to help learners to generate personal language • Give clear structure to learning – build in small steps on previous knowledge	• Learners can compile their own sets of 'picture prompts', use them to practise at home and support presentation in class • Use of Clicker grids and other software and on-line resources to reinforce vocabulary use

© Crombie, Thomson and McColl 2004 Presentation at British Dyslexia Conference, Warwick, March 2004

Further reading

CRIVELLI, V., THOMSON, M. AND ANDERSSEN, B. (2004) 'Using ICT to support dyslexia learners at secondary school', in G. Reid and A. Fawcett (eds) *Dyslexia in Context: Research, Policy and Practice*, London: Whurr.

CROMBIE, M. AND MCCOLL, H. (2001) 'Dyslexia and the teaching of modern foreign languages', in L. Peer and G. Reid (eds) *Dyslexia: Successful Inclusion in the Secondary School*, London: David Fulton.

CROMBIE, M. AND SCHNEIDER, E. (2004) *Dyslexia and Modern Foreign Languages: Gaining Success in an Inclusive Context*, London: David Fulton.

DARGIE, R. (2005) *Dyslexia and History*, London: David Fulton.

EADON, H. (2004) *Dyslexia and Drama*, London: David Fulton.

GRAY, R. (2001) 'Drama: the experience of learning', in L. Peer and G. Reid (eds) *Dyslexia: Successful Inclusion in the Secondary School*, London: David Fulton.

HENDERSON, A. (1998) *Maths for the Dyslexic: A Practical Guide*, London: David Fulton.

HOLMES, P. (2001) 'Dyslexia and Physics', in L. Peer and G. Reid (eds) *Dyslexia – Successful Inclusion in the Secondary School*, London: David Fulton.

HOWLETT, C.A. (2001) 'Dyslexia and Biology', in L. Peer and G. Reid (eds) *Dyslexia – Successful Inclusion in the Secondary School*, London: David Fulton.

KAY, J. AND YEO, D. (2003) *Dyslexia and Maths*, London: Taylor & Francis.

MILES, T. AND WESTCOMBE, J. (eds) (2001) *Music and Dyslexia: Opening New Doors*, London: Whurr.

OGLETHORPE, S. (2002) *Instrumental Music for Dyslexics: A Teaching Handbook*, London: Whurr.

OLIVER, J. (1999) *The Naked Chef*, London: Michael Joseph.

PORTWOOD, M. (2003) *Dyslexia and Physical Education*, London: David Fulton, pp. 81, 99.

REDGRAVE, S. AND BUZAN, T. (2001) *Head Strong: How to Get Physically and Mentally Fit*, London: HarperCollins.

RENALDI, F. (2003) *Dyslexia and Design & Technology*, London: David Fulton and the BDA.

WEST, T.G. (1997) *In the Mind's Eye*, Amherst, NY: Prometheus Books.

WILLIAMS, F. AND LEWIS, J. (2001) 'Dyslexia and Geography', in L. Peer and G. Reid (eds) *Dyslexia: Successful Inclusion in the Secondary School*, London: David Fulton.

CHAPTER 7

Dyslexia and examinations

In this chapter, readers will:

- examine the UK's Joint Council for Qualifications (JCQ) access arrangements for assessments, and the Scottish Qualifications Authority (SQA) alternative assessment arrangements available to dyslexic candidates;

- develop awareness of the key principles underpinning these arrangements;

- look at the conditions for eligibility for access/alternative arrangements and the evidence required;

- review access/alternative arrangements available for dyslexic students in National Curriculum testing;

- explore the range of access/alternative arrangements available, generally and for individual subjects;

- consider the impact of stress on exam performance;

- look at case studies to set exam arrangements for dyslexic candidates in context.

The arrangements discussed in this chapter refer to those published by the UK's Joint Council for Qualifications (JCQ) – and the Scottish Qualifications Authority (SQA). Access arrangements for assessments (alternative arrangements in Scotland) have previously been referred to as special examination arrangements or (inaccurately) as examination *accommodations* or *concessions*. Examination papers are not changed – or made easier – in any way and marking is the same for all candidates.

Access/alternative arrangements for assessment

Disability legislation requires examining bodies to make 'reasonable adjustments' to prevent placing disabled learners at a 'substantial disadvantage' compared to others, by reason of their disability. Access (alternative) arrangements for exams are also known as reasonable adjustments (QCA 2007b: 65; SQA 2004: 1–3).

Key principles

The purpose of access/alternative arrangements is to remove barriers to the demonstration of attainment by changing the delivery or method of assessments to make them accessible *without compromising the standards* (SQA 2004: 5). Examining bodies ensure that the process of assessment leading to certification is rigorous and fair, allowing candidates to demonstrate the skills and knowledge required for an award. Any access/alternative arrangements must not compromise the credibility of the award (JCQ 2007–8: 32) – they measure a specified activity against published standards and give consistent results.

Eligibility

Access/alternative arrangements should be based on the needs of individuals and on the demands of an assessment, not on disability – if a dyslexic student is able to achieve the required outcomes of a course of study, but is unable to demonstrate this in the usual way – then alternatives may be put in place (Thomson 2004: 1–2). If there is a marked discrepancy between a dyslexic student's subject ability and writing skills, a written exam may prevent accurate assessment, so an alternative arrangement – such as a scribe – may be requested (JCQ 2007–8: 12).

For dyslexic candidates, the examination itself is often a barrier to the demonstration of attainment. Dyslexic profiles may include difficulties related to reading and writing, problems with memory and organisation or difficulties created by placing time limits on examinations. If a dyslexic candidate is unable to read the examination paper within the time allowed, then the opportunity to demonstrate attainment is not being provided. Introducing additional time or a reader – electronic or human – to compensate for slow text processing may be requested to minimise this barrier. Schools should identify candidates' needs at an early stage, put support arrangements in place in the subject curriculum and discuss any proposed arrangements with the awarding body.

Evidence of need

Examining bodies require a current assessment report from an educational psychologist or from a teacher with specialist qualifications for identifying, assessing and teaching students with dyslexia. These reports do not have to be submitted, but must be available if required. SQA (2004: 10) does not require a new assessment of a student's dyslexia if this already exists, but an educational psychologist might be expected to verify the need for any assessment arrangement requests.

Evidence is required showing that the school has made provision for dyslexic candidates during the course leading up to the exams. An evidence file showing resources committed to supporting individuals in subject classrooms will probably already exist, containing information from teachers about the nature and level of support that each student receives in a subject. Support needs vary in different subjects and at different levels – decisions about access/alternative arrangements should be made on a subject by subject basis, based on information from teachers about *actual* support needed for dyslexic students to overcome barriers to demonstration of attainment.

Quality assurance

When a dyslexic exam candidate is placed at a substantial disadvantage and adjustments are considered, SQA (2004: 9) suggests a four-step process for internal quality assurance:

- subject and specialist dyslexia teachers identify needs;

- candidate and subject teachers select appropriate alternatives;

- educational psychologist and specialist dyslexia teachers verify the need for the alternative format;

- head teachers authorise requests.

In Scotland, Quality Assurance Managers monitor a sample of centres each year to ensure that they have effective internal systems and procedures for requesting reasonable adjustments (SQA 2004: 15). Acceptable evidence might include an existing working file – such as an Individualised Educational Programme – and minutes of meetings.

JCQ quality assurance is embedded in the paperwork required for applications for access arrangements (2007–8: 62–82) and includes criteria for approval of specialist teachers' qualifications, preparing reports (2007–8: 37–8) and detailed advice for linking literacy attainment to access arrangements (2007–8: 34–6).

Access/alternative arrangements for national testing

England, Wales and NI, Key Stages; Scotland, 5–14 levels

National curriculum tests are not external examinations but instruments designed to confirm a teacher's continuous assessment of student progress in relation to national standards. These should not be confused with standardised tests or public exams where arrangements may be very different.

When taking national tests, dyslexic students should be given the same level of support that they normally receive in the classroom (except for some tests of reading and writing). This should be no more than is necessary to allow them to demonstrate their levels of attainment in the subjects being tested. Arrangements do not provide any advantage, the support does not change test questions and answers are the student's own.

Permitted arrangements for dyslexic students in national tests are similar to those available for public exams – e.g. extra time is usually 25 per cent – but there are differences:

- Assistance may be provided with reading the instructions and the questions – but not the text in a reading assessment in Scotland.

- In England, Wales and Northern Ireland, no aspect of a reading or Shakespeare paper should be read to a student other than general instructions.

- A scribe or ICT may be used (except to test handwriting and presentation), but when spelling/punctuation are to be assessed in English writing tests students should dictate punctuation as well as words and the spellchecker should be disabled.

- If it will be difficult for a marker to read a student's writing, scripts may be transcribed.

- Tests may be scanned into a computer for use with a screen reader and other specialised reading/writing software that is normally used in class.

- Enlarged print version of tests may be ordered – or tests copied on coloured paper and tinted overlays or filter lenses used if this is normal classroom practice.

Readers for Mathematics and Science tests

In Mathematics and Science tests, readers may:

- name signs, symbols and numbers;

- read back responses;

- clarify text in a question as long as no clue is given to the answer;

- refer students back to the previous part of multipart questions.

Scribes for National Curriculum tests

Alternatives to using scribes should be provided where possible. Scribes should:

- ensure that language, punctuation and phrasing are students' own;

- not expect spellings to be dictated;

- work at students' own pace and allow time for reflection, reading or rest;

- follow students' instructions precisely for drawing diagrams, charts and graphs;

- ask students to dictate punctuation in English writing tests.

Additional arrangements

- Schools may enhance the shading on diagrams, charts and graphs, to increase their visual clarity;

- diagrams may be enlarged if care is taken to avoid changing the nature of any question, particularly in mathematics.

Approval for access/alternative arrangements for National Curriculum testing

Approval from the NAA National Curriculum tests or the SQA 5–14 Assessment Unit for access/alternative arrangements is not required but these bodies can be approached if clarification is needed.

Records of all access/alternative arrangements used should be kept and students' records annotated to indicate any support used. Evidence files supporting the provision of access/alternative arrangements should be kept by primary schools and passed on at transition.

Details of any access/alternative arrangements proposed for assessments and timed tests should always be shared with parents and students.

Available access/alternative arrangements

Some access/alternative arrangements required by dyslexic candidates may be relatively simple to implement, having little impact on the learning outcomes being assessed – e.g. use of flexible deadlines for submission of course work or work being submitted in an alternative format to writing. At school level, the use of a word processor for coursework is acceptable from all candidates, making dyslexic candidate scripts more accessible to markers, removing the 'fatigue' factor implicit in marking illegible examination scripts (Cogan and Flecker 2004: 288). Schools may permit candidates to use coloured overlays on the paper without seeking permission, though invigilators should be advised in advance.

Examining bodies offer a number of arrangements for dyslexic students that apply to coursework, internal assessments and terminal examinations. These include:

- linguistic support (reader, scribe, transcription with correction, digital exam papers);

- extra time allowances;

- use of ICT – word processors with spellcheckers/specialised software;

- transcription without correction to remove illegibility;

- rest periods/supervised breaks when extra time makes an exam extremely long;

- adapted question papers for candidates who experience visual distortions.

All examination scripts are marked against set criteria but for some subjects it may be possible to refer dyslexic students' scripts to the Principal Assessor for an opinion. This does not mean that set criteria are changed in any way but some scripts may be difficult for a marker to interpret and the opinion of the Principal Assessor could provide useful guidance (SQA 2004: 27).

Internal assessments

When an internal assessment involves substantial reading and writing, dyslexic candidates are eligible for the same linguistic support used in class and for timed exams.

Some dyslexic students may require additional arrangements for school-based assessments that do not fall into the broad categories given in the guidelines, e.g. if the assessment instructions are given orally, dyslexic students may need to have these repeated. Schools wishing to provide such arrangements should request permission from the awarding body, giving details of their use for subject coursework.

Assessments of practical skills

Unless they have a co-morbid condition affecting motor skills, few dyslexic students will be eligible for a helper in practical assessments (JCQ 2007–8: 13–14). This arrangement will not be available where the practical skill is the focus of the examination but there are arrangements that might be required to reflect normal working, e.g. some dyslexic candidates may be given a large-print version of instructions, or ask for specific seating/work station arrangements in order to take account of ambient lighting.

Linguistic support

Examining bodies provide detailed advice and exemplars of the use of the permitted access/alternative arrangements. (JCQ 2007–8: 4–28; SQA 2004: 19–24). The possible arrangements available are very wide, and teachers should advise the use of those that reflect the support or strategies already in place. Dyslexic candidates will not need the same arrangement for every assessment – a reader or extra time allowance may be needed for an examination that contains lengthy text passages, but not for one where the reading content is comparatively slight.

EAL dyslexic students

A reader will not be allowed if a candidate's literacy difficulties are primarily caused by English not being their first language. Candidates who have been in the UK for less than two years and for whom English is an additional language cannot have a reader unless a history of need and provision can be established in their first language or a dyslexic profile has been identified. When dyslexia is clearly established, an EAL candidate will be eligible for both dyslexic and bilingual arrangements. However, even when translation of subject content into the first language is normal practice in the curriculum, exams are certificated with English as the carrier language, so this cannot be changed.

Extra time allowances

There should be evidence from subject teachers that the candidate normally lags behind classmates in completion of set tasks. Evidence from standardised tests of reading and/or dyslexia assessment instruments that indicate reading rate also show any need for additional time – up to 25 per cent extra is usually permitted, according to individual needs.

The technique sometimes employed by those assessing dyslexia when carrying out a standardised test within a time limit, can be a useful tool for determining how much extra time might be appropriate for an individual – provided this is carried out in a non-examination setting. The dyslexic candidate would proceed with the test and when the permitted time is up, either record the time by annotating the paper, or perhaps change pens and continue using a different colour. Not only can the amount of time needed to complete the test be measured but the candidate's use of any additional time can be observed – e.g. to continue answering, to check answers, to complete questions missed out. It is important to stress that this technique should *never* be used during an actual assessment, as this would invalidate any results.

Case study: Sara, age 15 – extra time for exams

The educational psychologist's report recommended extra time provision for several activities, including timed exams. The school did not have a specialist dyslexia teacher and access arrangements were managed by a member of the special needs team who decided to use the 'changing pen colour' method to measure how much extra time would be required for Sara in exams. When mock exams took place, Sara was asked to stay behind after the other students had left the exam hall, given a different pen and allowed 25 per cent more time. Her exam scripts were marked up to the change of pen, then the extra bit was marked, and the 'extra' marks evaluated. Not surprisingly, she did not gain very many more marks in the extra time, so it was concluded that extra time did not make a difference to her performance and no application was made for access arrangements.

Sara's parents consulted the Disability Rights Commission who agreed that this was discriminatory practice and a failure to make reasonable adjustments.

It is not appropriate to assess candidates' eligibility for extra time allowances by measuring only what they can produce in additional time added at the end of a formal examination. The need for extra time is related to the speed of processing language and accessing stored information as well as to difficulties putting thoughts into words and sequencing them appropriately, so this method of determining a discrepancy is seriously flawed, as well as being potentially damaging to the self-esteem of the candidate.

A dyslexic candidate's work rate will be known by subject teachers, who should have little difficulty producing evidence showing the need for extra time allowances. Many subject teachers prepare students for examinations by giving class tests and these could easily be used to assess how much extra time is required for a dyslexic student. The actual extra time required by individuals is often impossible to quantify, since the content of the examination paper bears directly on this, so subject teachers should suggest what they believe to be appropriate for individuals in their own subject (JCQ 2007–8: 5).

Use of a reader

A reader is allowed in subjects where a candidate has difficulty accessing written text within a set time. Evidence required may consist of standardised test scores indicating reading speed and accuracy well below the expected level (JCA 2007: 80), or details and examples of subject work done with and without a reader showing a clear discrepancy between these. If a candidate is able to access text in the curriculum but still requests a reader, submission of evidence may be required.

Case study: Michael, age 16 – reader for exams

Michael's dyslexia was known and supported across the curriculum, and there was ample evidence that his reading rate was so slow that the extra time allowance was not enough to compensate for the lengthy reading in history exams. The history teacher, however, reported that Michael did not need support for reading in class and allowing a reader for an exam did not reflect his usual way of working, identifying writing as the major difficulty and this was supported by the use of ICT. Concerned, the dyslexia specialist sat in on a few history lessons to evaluate the support provided for Michael and discovered that the teacher read all text aloud to the class.

After consideration, Michael agreed to use a text reader and a word processor, with extra time in the history exam to meet his identified needs and more closely reflect support in class.

It is common for dyslexic students to request more than one arrangement for a single exam and teachers should note that a reader is not a scribe – though the same person may act as both as long as permission has been given for both arrangements.

Use of a scribe

To qualify for this arrangement, the candidate must normally have difficulty producing written responses at an appropriate level (Thomson 2004: 3). There should be evidence of a real difference between the content, quality, and speed of output when the candidate dictates as opposed to free writing (JCQ 2007–8: 9–12; 81). This might include details of any assessment of speed, accuracy and legibility of writing contributed by a subject teacher; spelling assessments; comparisons between the speed of free writing and dictated/copied writing (or word processing). If a candidate can normally produce written work of an acceptable standard and a scribe is still requested, evidence of the reasons for this would be required prior to approval (JCQ 2007–8: 12 example V). A candidate with writing difficulties might not be placed at any substantial disadvantage in a subject assessment with limited writing, such as a multiple-choice question paper but the same candidate might experience difficulties in an assessment that requires the production of an essay.

Transcription

This arrangement would be requested where a candidate's handwriting is so difficult to read that it would be beneficial for an examiner to be able to refer to a transcript for clarification (JCQ 2007–8: 19). Evidence for this would be much the same as required for a scribe, possibly including examples of illegible writing in each subject concerned. In some cases, where dyslexic spelling takes a marker time to decipher, the transcript could correct spelling (JCQ 2007–8: 20, example 2).

Use of ICT

ICT may be requested by dyslexic students for exams in subjects where they normally use it, but restrictions may apply to some applications in some subject examinations. Where additional arrangements such as extra time, use of spellchecker or particular software are requested, schools must have evidence to show these are routinely used.

Pupils with writing difficulties who normally use a word processor will be eligible to use this for written exams. Where there are set criteria for spelling and punctuation, word processor tools that help with these must be switched off and scripts are marked accordingly. In subjects where there are no specific criteria that affect spelling and grammar, candidates may apply to use the same software normally provided in class. Voice-activated software may be used – with editorial functions turned off if necessary. If predictive software is normal classroom practice, it may be used in some exams, but the word bank from which the words are drawn must be no shorter than an average-sized school dictionary – it is not acceptable to use packages that rely solely on word lists created by teachers.

Use of computer software to read out a scanned paper – but not to interpret it – may be used as a reader, using the same criteria and evidence of need. In the same way, digital exam papers can provide support for both reading and writing, though the evidence of the use of these in the curriculum may be scarce, as they are not yet readily available (Nisbet *et al.* 2006: 7, 35).

Other arrangements

There are a number of access/alternative arrangements that may be available for a small number of dyslexic candidates – some may be put in place if the dyslexic student has a co-morbid condition, e.g. a prompter when ADHD or epilepsy is also present (SQA 2004: 27; JCQ 2007–8: 21–2). Others may be subject-specific and have to be negotiated with the examining body, including:

- rest periods/supervised breaks where extra time makes a paper very long;

- adapted question papers for candidates with visual processing deficits, e.g. papers printed on different colours or enlarged print papers;

- use of technological support such as the use of spelling aids or calculator use in non-calculator Maths papers.

(Thomson 2007f: 14)

These must reflect the support provided for dyslexic students in the curriculum and address specific difficulties caused by the style of the examination.

Use of access/alternative arrangements previously does not mean that these will automatically be granted again – subject- and course-based evidence of on-going support will be required for every application for access/alternative arrangements for each examination diet.

Arrangements for subject assessments

The arrangements applied to a subject assessment should match the support provided for course work in that subject. However, a dyslexic learner may be able to cope with the reading demands of a subject with extra time allowances in class, but a reader is needed in a timed examination because the amount of extra time required to process the text is in excess of that permitted, or would make the exam paper so long that fatigue becomes a limiting factor.

A candidate will not require the same arrangements for all assessments. Different subjects and different methods of assessment make different demands and some access/alternative arrangements permitted for one type of assessment may not be permitted for others – e.g. extra time will not be permitted in exams testing the time in which a practical skill is performed, such as keyboarding, musical performance or expressive arts, where the timing may be a crucial part of the assessment.

Art, Craft & Design

Few dyslexic students request access/alternative arrangements for practical assessments in Art, Craft & Design, but many will need these for timed, written exams.

Drama

Dyslexic students may request access/alternative arrangements for internal assessments that involve making notes or reading to prepare for an activity, e.g. script production.

English

Arrangements permitted in Scotland by SQA differ from those allowed in the rest of the UK. SQA allows the use of readers, scribes, ICT and transcription for all English papers – though there are restrictions when criteria for spelling and grammar are applied.

JCQ does not allow a reader in sections of English papers testing reading, such as GCSE English Literature or combined Language/Literature specifications. Dyslexic candidates normally eligible for readers but not permitted this arrangement may apply for an extra time allowance greater than 25 per cent.

Information and Communications Technology

Some dyslexic students may require access/alternative arrangements in practical assessments for reading and spelling, when difficulties prevent practical activities being carried out. A spellchecker or prompt sheet may be requested if spelling is not being assessed. Access/alternative arrangements will not normally be permitted for keyboarding assessments where there are set criteria for speed and accuracy, though exam papers may be adapted and screen filters will be allowed.

Maths

Examining bodies offer the same range of access/alternative arrangements for Maths exams as for all other subjects – and some additional arrangements may be provided specifically for maths assessments, to reflect support in the classroom – e.g. adapted exam papers where graphs are enlarged for those who experience visual processing difficulties or the use of tables squares in non-calculator papers.

Modern Foreign Languages

Many dyslexic students reject access/alternative arrangements for speaking assessments, but this is less likely to be the case when timed exams are required.

In Scotland readers and scribes may be requested for assessments in Modern Foreign Languages (or Gaelic) but where the overall quality of the written language, particularly spelling accuracy, is being assessed, a scribe must follow explicit instructions from the candidate with regard to spelling and/or the placement of accents. A scribe cannot assume that the candidate knows how to spell a word/phrase in the foreign language and must request clarification if a candidate's dictation is unclear. Transcription with correction is not permitted in the assessment of writing where the overall quality of the written language, particularly spelling accuracy, is being assessed (SQA 2004: 36–7).

In the rest of the UK, for exams in Irish (or Gaeilge), Welsh, Modern Foreign Languages, a reader is not permitted for reading papers, nor a scribe or transcription with correction for writing papers, though additional extra time may be allowed.

Access/alternative arrangements for Modern Foreign Language assessments may include making particular adjustments when listening and writing are being assessed:

- When pre-recorded materials are used for listening tests, extra time may be built in to take account of the slower language processing of dyslexic students.

- When ICT is requested for writing in the target language, permission may be requested for other language software use.

- When listening to instructions in the target language or English dyslexic students may request them repeated.

Music

The Associated Board of the Royal Schools of Music (2005) have established guidelines for dyslexic candidates in Grade examinations. Other examining bodies offer the same range of access/alternative assessment arrangements for all subjects but:

- Tapes for listening tests may have extra time or repeated questions included.

- Extra time may not be permitted for a practical music examination despite the need for reading of musical notation – e.g. sight-reading may be tested within strict time limits.

- Those who experience visual processing difficulties may request adapted musical notations to prevent 'clumping' of notes, making them impossible to distinguish.

Physical Education

When video tapes are used in examinations extra time between sections and the opportunity for questions to be repeated may be requested.

Science

Some dyslexic students may require access/alternative arrangements for practical assessments as well as in timed, written exams:

- graphs and tables may be enlarged;

- formulae prompts may be requested when these are not issued to all.

Social subjects

Exams in, for example, History and Modern Studies may involve a lot of reading and writing, so some dyslexic students who have coped in the classroom with minimal support may require more extensive access/alternative arrangements than anticipated. In addition:

- picture sources may be enlarged;

- overlays may be used when, for example, Geography maps cannot be produced on coloured paper.

Exams and stress

The combination of low self-esteem and stress affects performance in examinations – if students expect to perform badly, they probably will. Matching access/assessment arrangements to the curriculum support that meets the needs of individuals will help to reduce the effects of stress. However, many dyslexic students do not wish to be different from their classmates, so when access/alternative arrangements are offered, they may reject them. Preparation for assessments must include measures to improve dyslexic candidates' confidence, with opportunities to practice using any agreed arrangements.

At all stages of education dyslexic learners should have access to appropriate support and access/alternative arrangements that enable them to reveal their actual ability and to achieve certification at an appropriate level.

Further reading

BACKHOUSE, G., DOLMAN, E. AND READ, C. (edited by Greenwald) (2007) *Dyslexia: Assessing the Need for Access Arrangements during Examinations: a Practical Guide* (3rd edn), Evesham, Worcs: PATOSS & JCQ.

UNIVERSITY OF EDINBURGH with The CALL Centre (2007) *Accessible Digital Exams* retrieved 10 July 2007 from www.callcentresscotland.org/digitalexams/.

CHAPTER 8

Developing independent study skills

In this chapter, readers will:

- develop awareness of how secondary students acquire study skills;

- review teaching styles and dyslexic students' learning preferences;

- explore barriers for dyslexic students to effective study – e.g. weak reading skills, difficulty with writing – and consider how to reduce these;

- understand the role of note taking in the curriculum and how this may affect dyslexic students' learning;

- look at ways of supporting dyslexic students' short-term memory problems affecting the organisation and processing of information;

- consider how dyslexic students might approach revision;

- become aware of the support needed by many dyslexic students to access the school library.

Acquiring study skills

Dyslexic students often lack confidence in their ability to learn and have an expectation of failure – not only because of prior experience of struggling with literacy but also because they may not have developed the under-pinning study skills of independent learners. The acquisition of subject-specific study skills in the secondary curriculum is largely incidental; during normal delivery of their subjects, teachers model required responses and advise students on revision. Few dyslexic students can access this type of input – they often lack the energy or time to absorb incidental comments or to reproduce techniques explained by teachers 'in passing'.

Teaching styles

Learning effectively is hard work for all students and some will have difficulty learning because of the way they are being taught. The way in which the curriculum is delivered by subject teachers is an important factor in students' learning, and may create barriers for some dyslexic students. When there is a mismatch between a teacher's preferred style and a student's learning preference, learning is likely to be incomplete and concentration may be difficult in that class (Ostler 2000: 3).

No single teaching style appears to be 'most' effective. Many teachers deliver the curriculum by talking – not always effective for dyslexic students, whose slower processing of auditory input causes them to lose the thread and become confused when trying to make sense of lesson content. Teachers who have a visual preference should remember that it is unlikely that dyslexic students will be able to create their own versions of mind maps or diagrams unless these are specifically taught.

Many subject teachers are aware of the need to vary their style of curriculum delivery and have developed ways of working with learners drawing from a number of different approaches or sources. Even when standard programmes of work are used, teachers make their own adaptations in order to ensure that their students can access the materials (Reid and Green 2007: 56–7).

Learning preferences

Not all students with dyslexia will learn in the same way – some are intuitive learners who like discussion and practical activities that allow them to try out various options while others prefer a more systematic step-by-step approach (Henderson *et al.* 2003: 124). Problems with literacy may lead to some dyslexic students developing unconventional coping strategies and ways of thinking, and they should be encouraged to explore their own learning styles to identify strengths.

Some characteristics of learning styles are fairly easy to identify (Thomson 2006: 53; and see **Photocopiables 8.1** (p. 141) and **8.2** (p. 142). Visual learners remember best what they see, auditory–verbal learners get more out of words, and tactile/kinaesthetic learners learn best by manipulating objects. The Given and Reid (1999) model extends this to include social and emotional factors:

- physical – need to do;
- cognitive – need to know;
- reflective – need to reflect;
- emotional – need to be;
- social – need to belong.

Their model of the cognitive learning cycle (1999: 56) illustrating how information is perceived, remembered and expressed may be useful to subject teachers who are puzzled by the apparently random learning styles of dyslexic students.

Having a strong preference for one learning style does not mean that students are unable to use features of other styles (Chinn in Peer and Reid 2001: 117–18). Although dyslexic students may lack flexibility, many adapt their approaches to learning to suit the demands of different subjects and to teachers' delivery styles, especially as they get older. Honey and Mumford (1986) divide learners into four distinct groups according to preference:

- action – doing/experiencing something;

- reflection – thinking about/reviewing what has been done;

- theorising – drawing conclusions based on the previous stages;

- pragmatism – planning/deciding what to do next.

Any learning styles approach to support provision for dyslexic students emphasises matching teaching to learning preferences, using student's strengths to maximise learning and to support specific weaknesses.

Gathering information

Although dyslexic students struggle to obtain information from visual or aural lessons they often compensate by adjusting their learning styles to match subject teachers' delivery methods. A major source of information in the secondary curriculum is the study of subject texts, materials and notes, and dyslexic students' reading difficulties will be a barrier to effective study and learning (see **Photocopiable 8.3** on p. 143 for advice on making information more accessible to dyslexic students). Those who have a history of slow, inaccurate reading may have a single strategy for study – reading one word at a time. This can slow reading so much that meaning is lost altogether, so different strategies will be needed for different reading tasks (Ostler 2000: 35; Turner and Pughe 2003: 7).

Reading for information

When the purpose of reading is to find out something, dyslexic students should first note down what it is they are looking for – highlighting the key words – then scan the page until they find these words. It is not necessary to read anything when scanning, and with practice, even very slow readers can learn to do this – eventually (Reid and Green 2007: 60).

Reading instructions

If the purpose of reading is to follow instructions, dyslexic readers may have to read word by word, perhaps several times. It might be useful for them to scan the instructions first to locate key words, e.g. look for the word 'equipment', then to read that section closely to find out, for example, if equipment has to be collected. This would help students to break instructions into smaller segments that are easier to manage. When an activity requires a long series of instructions, teachers might issue checklists to dyslexic students who could tick each step as it is completed – this would not only help them follow instructions in the correct order but ensure that no steps are accidentally missed or repeated.

Study reading

Barriers to reading experienced by dyslexic students are likely to be linked to reading speed and accuracy, losing the place and forgetting what has just been read. Many teachers use direct activities related to texts (DARTs) to help dyslexic students engage with particular aspects of text, perhaps stopping reading after each paragraph to note key ideas or completing cloze exercises to reinforce understanding.

Study reading is difficult for dyslexic students, as it requires a combination of reading and remembering. McKay (2005: 140–1) offers a *Dyslexia Friendly Strategy for Study Reading* involving looking at the whole text before seeking answers to specific questions, while Ostler and Ward (2001: 33–4) explore SQ3R – Surveying the material, Questioning what information is needed then Reading the text (more than once) and checking Recall. Once this process has been completed, it is Reviewed and its usefulness determined. SQ3R = Survey – Question – Read – Recall – Review (see **Photocopiable 8.4** on p. 144 for another version of this technique).

Recording information: note-taking

Note-taking is an important study skill that enables students to review what they have learned and to revise for exams. Teachers use various ways of developing students' skills – notes may be copied from the board, dictated or have to be made while students listen/watch during a lesson – all of which will be difficult for dyslexic students. Subject teachers should explain the process and purpose of note-taking and demonstrate any required format – but take account of students' learning preferences and permit some variations. Auditory learners often use a linear style written from left to right, from the top of the page to the bottom, identifying key words to trigger mental images of concepts and ideas (Ostler and Ward 2004: 45). Visual learners prefer to show ideas using mind maps, charts and drawings whereas others prefer highlighting and coloured presentations of key concepts, images and important definitions (Cogan and Flecker 2004: 132–4).

Skeleton notes

Teachers might provide dyslexic students with skeleton notes in advance – giving the headings of content to be covered in a lesson – to support note-taking, but some will remember nothing of the lesson if they have to concentrate on completing notes (Cogan and Flecker 2004: 117). These students could be given prompt cards summarising key points or full lesson notes, and highlight key points while listening to the teacher instead of completing a skeleton.

Visual notes

Some dyslexic students spend an inordinate amount of time creating tables and diagrams – teachers might issue these as blanks so that more time is available for entering data and labelling accurately. When tables, diagrams and spider graphs/Mind Maps (© Buzan) are required, their construction should be taught so that students are able to create and retrieve information from them. Spider graphs/mind maps are a way of recording ideas showing the links between them as they arise – using drawings or words, according to preference. Using such 'maps' enables students to capture and organise what they want to write without worrying about how to write it.

Notes on text

Dyslexic students will take much longer than others to make notes from books and find it difficult to decide what is essential, so end up copying lengthy passages. Photocopying sections or using a personal copy of a book allows key text to be highlighted and annotated instead. If dyslexic students find it difficult to annotate text appropriately – perhaps due to losing the place often – enlarging a copy of the page will make this easier.

When annotation is not possible, students should be advised that main points are usually found in the first and last sentences of paragraphs. Many textbooks summarise key ideas and content at the start or end of chapters and these could provide a useful structure for personal notes.

Recording notes

For those students whose dyslexia is severe, the use of a recorder might be encouraged. Teachers' spoken input could be recorded for later transcription or stored as voice files for revision. If teachers are uncomfortable with this, they could issue a pre-recorded version, which would be clear and to the point, although any added explanations and responses to queries would be missed.

Organisation of information

Dyslexic students will always struggle with note-taking to some extent and many will require additional support as well as explicit teaching of techniques. Some subject teachers issue notebooks and give guidelines for setting out work; if this is not done, dyslexic students' layout and organisation of notes on the page may be messy and incomprehensible. When loose-leaf folders are used and dyslexic students decide for themselves how to store notes – chronological, alphabetical or topical – they will need frequent reminders about the importance of labelling and dating notes, and additional reminders and support for organising notes in sequence (Cogan and Flecker 2004: 149). Whatever system is used, space should be available for updating and adding to notes. Some students transfer notes to a computer and they should make sure that files are properly named and that they have a back-up in case of any malfunction.

Processing information: memory

It is important not to view dyslexia simply as a literacy difficulty – dyslexic students may not readily consolidate new learning and are likely to need more input before they can remember particular teaching points. Even when a skill has apparently been learnt, it may be lost if there is interference from competing activities – e.g. a student may know how to spell a word when he thinks about it but the spelling will break down when he writes it while thinking about sequence. Dyslexic students must over-learn much of the curriculum and subject teachers should arrange repeated practice to ensure that learning points are consolidated and transferred to long-term memory (Reid 2004: 61–2).

Inefficient working memory has long been implicated as an underlying factor in dyslexia. Dyslexic students may have difficulty maintaining material in temporary memory storage while carrying out another skill (Kay and Yeo 2003: 14–15) so a student who has to focus on decoding letter–sound links, has less attention available for the process of understanding what has been read. Reid and Green (2007: 14–15) suggest that teachers model and provide practice in techniques for students to monitor comprehension.

Many dyslexic students do not easily attach verbal labels to pictures and have difficulties with lists, so they compensate by relying on visual codes for memory processing – they may recognise faces but be unable to remember names, and recognise landmarks but struggle to give or follow directions to get there. McKay (2005: 144–9) suggests that dyslexic students may learn to remember by identifying their own learning preferences and transforming information from one form to their preferred style. Strategies for improving memory are as varied as the teachers promoting them, ranging from singing multiplication tables to imagining a fantastic journey – and dyslexic students should adopt whatever technique works for them.

Presentation of information: writing

It may be difficult for dyslexic students to plan written work and follow an ordered sequence in the development of ideas. In some subjects, such as English, teachers actually teach how to write essays of different types and give students a framework, structured prompt or template to support writing in different formats, e.g. giving an opening phrase for each paragraph and suggested vocabulary (Reid and Green 2007: 65–6).

There may be an assumption in some subject areas that students already know how to produce structured written responses, and some subject teachers do not see it as their responsibility to teach this. However, no matter what the experience and skills of the rest of the class, dyslexic students need specific instruction in how to structure written work, as they may be unable to transfer skills acquired in one subject to a different context.

Scaffolding (McKay 2005: 58) is a flexible way of providing writing support to dyslexic students, involving several stages that might be gradually withdrawn as confidence and skills develop. Support provided includes:

- help with planning writing, freeing students to compose without constraint – using recorders, computers, or scribes;

- provision of lists of sentence starters/key words;

- writing frames or story skeletons to be expanded;

- modelling the required written work.

Editing and redrafting

Redrafting is very different from rewriting and should be taught as a specific skill (Turner and Pughe 2003: 64–5). Many dyslexic students dread redrafting, thinking that they have to rewrite their work, but this is not so – redrafting involves a critical appraisal of the writing to determine whether it actually responds to the question or follows the writing plan, then making only changes that will improve the quality of the piece.

Dyslexic students should be encouraged to separate the process of proofreading from that of writing and redrafting. Teachers should allow time between these activities, and give explicit instructions about how to proofread rather than just telling students to 'read over' their work. Proofreading may be done for different purposes – to check content and organisation, to consider grammar, expression and sentence structure, and to check spelling. Dyslexic students who write using a computer may take different approaches, according to the software used. Teachers should be cautious about encouraging students to proofread each other's work as this may place those who are dyslexic at risk of public humiliation.

Further reading

GRIFFITHS, M. (2002) *Study Skills and Dyslexia in the Secondary School: A Practical Approach*, London: David Fulton.

HONEY, P. AND MUMFORD, A. (1986) *The Manual of Learning Styles*, Maidenhead: Peter Honey Publications.

CHAPTER 9

Using ICT to support dyslexia

In this chapter, readers will:

- look at the role of ICT use to support dyslexia in the subject curriculum;

- explore the use of ICT to support dyslexic students' developing literacy;

- look at a case study to set dyslexia and ICT in context;

- consider some barriers created by teachers to dyslexic students' use of laptop computers in the classroom;

- become aware of the potential advantages of speech recognition software for dyslexic students;

- review the use of ICT by dyslexic students in exams.

Possibly the single most important support strategy for dyslexic students in the secondary curriculum is the use of Information and Communications Technology (Crivelli in Peer and Reid 2001: 219). Secondary subject teachers are well aware of the impact of technology on how students research and present homework and projects, but for many dyslexic students, ICT use is not just a way of removing the stigma of poor spelling and handwriting, it cuts through layers of obstacles that previously prevented them from demonstrating their actual ability (Cogan and Flecker 2004: 71).

ICT for writing

Writing is a frustrating experience for dyslexic students who are unable to begin to write down the words they wish to use to express themselves. Using a word processor removes many of the barriers they experience with handwriting – poorly formed letters, slow writing rate and weak spelling

(Nisbet *et al.* 1999: 14) – and frees dyslexic students to concentrate on the content of writing providing the opportunity to become more organised. Word processing packages are usually context free, so can be used across the curriculum, together with bolt-on programs for dyslexic use that will enable the addition of word banks or predictive lexicons to support subject vocabulary and spelling. Spellcheckers allow the flow of writing to progress without being interrupted by inability to spell appropriate vocabulary, and enables the dyslexic, finally, to demonstrate subject knowledge and ability more appropriately. Written work may be easily edited and re-sequenced without the need to write it all over again and the dyslexic student may then be given help and guidance appropriate to content rather than teachers' attention being focused on the quality of written language (Thomson in Reid and Fawcett 2004: 312). Since it is the editing stage of word processing when adult support is most needed by dyslexic students, this can be arranged for later so students do not have to wait for teacher attention in order to complete written work.

ICT for reading

Difficulties accessing and reading books and other materials have a huge impact on dyslexic students' opportunities to become successful learners. It is very difficult for students whose reading lacks fluency, or whose decoding is such a struggle that they cannot remember what they have just 'read', to enjoy fiction. Audio books have often been used to give dyslexic students access to literature, and ICT makes books available on CD-ROM and on-line. Text to speech (or screen reading) software provides dyslexic students access to a wealth of text materials, and interactive packages that respond to prompts by the reader require only minimal teacher intervention, increasing the independence of the dyslexic reader. UK copyright legislation (Copyright (Visually Impaired Persons) Act 2002) currently permits adaptation and distribution of digital texts for people who are visually impaired without requiring permission from the publisher, but this is not generally available for dyslexic students, and teachers must seek permission for every book, for each individual student, and it is illegal to share books and materials (Nisbet and Aitken 2007: 3).

ICT for drawing

Some subjects require the use of highly specialised software, e.g. computer-aided design, and this must be specifically taught by subject teachers to all students. Most computer applications offer drawing tools for producing diagrams, but many students will be slow and clumsy with these to begin with – so they need lots of practice in order to develop this skill. Some dyslexic students prefer to draw diagrams by hand and insert them into printed work or scan them into the computer for incorporation into text, but this can take a long time, and may not always be possible especially in exams. Using a spreadsheet alongside a word processor makes the production of tables and graphs much easier, as these can be copied from one application to the other.

Search skills

Using dictionaries and other reference books is frustrating for dyslexic students as the sheer volume of text on the printed page often makes it impossible for them to find anything. Many dictionaries and encyclopaedias are now available on-line or as CD-ROMs – some with speech output that reduces the need for sophisticated reading skills. These aids still require some reading/spelling skills, but it is possible for dyslexic students to concentrate on the use of key words when searching for information. Using the Internet to find information has been very difficult for dyslexic students who could not spell the search terminology – but Google corrects spelling errors making locating information easier. All Internet users need to be able to scan information to determine whether it is relevant to the topic they are researching, and this can be a very demanding task for dyslexic students, but the use of text-to-speech software makes it possible for them to evaluate text files fairly easily.

Some dyslexic students fail to engage with aspects of the secondary subject curriculum because of a lack of underpinning literacy skills, which is frustrating and may be humiliating and contribute to low self-esteem; ICT provides a multi-sensory learning environment that eliminates the expectation of failure and re-motivates them, boosting their self-confidence and improving their access to the curriculum without having to make frequent requests for individual help in the classroom, finally allowing them to become independent learners (Crivelli in Peer and Reid 2001: 218–19).

Case study: Bradley, age 11 – training in ICT

Bradley had been assessed as being exceptionally able at primary school but his reading and writing skills were very poor due to dyslexia, and a learning assistant had been provided in the classroom to support his access to the curriculum by reading and scribing for him. Although this worked well in his primary school where his ability and difficulties were well known, there were concerns about what might happen in a bigger school with a lot more teachers who did not know him.

An individualised transition programme was arranged for Bradley and during his final year of primary education he spent a half day every week in the secondary school. At first, the dyslexia specialist found it difficult to understand him – he spoke very fast with an odd accent, but the educational psychologist explained that this was because his speech could not keep up with his speed of thought. Secondary staff found that his attention span during reading activities was very short; his dictated work was correct but extremely brief. Analysis of these revealed that reading activities had been very slow – to accommodate his word-by-word decoding – and his dictation speed was limited by the writing rate of his scribe.

ICT had been tried at primary but rejected – when given an AlphaSmart laptop Bradley had not written much more than he produced by hand but took twice as long, although the spelling was better and the work was legible. He was reluctant to participate in class computer activities and rejected the laptop. His parents commented that he enjoyed using his brother's Play Station and was very good at some games.

It was agreed that the secondary team would try again with ICT. Bradley was exposed to a number of different desktop computers and a wide range of specialised dyslexia software. It was noted that his mouse skills were very good but that he had few keyboard skills; he responded very well when instructions were spoken but was slow to react if keyboard responses were required; he enjoyed the challenges offered in literacy and numeracy 'games'. He was placed on a keyboarding skills programme that used a games approach and he continued to use the numeracy and literacy software he liked. This software was loaded on to a PC laptop so that he could use it daily in his primary classroom. He enjoyed the software so much that he started using it at home and his progress was remarkable – in a very few weeks he became a skilled computer operator, with very fast, accurate keyboarding, and his attainments in literacy and numeracy were considerable. The laptop he was using had a word processing package, and he started using this for written work without any instruction – stunning his primary teacher when he handed in a well presented lengthy (for him) piece of writing. The secondary team immediately introduced him to other word processing packages that offered support and to 'extras' that would work with the software he was already using – and started him on word processing lessons to teach text editing.

The next review considered his remarkable progress – easily commensurate with his very high ability – and questioned what had gone wrong in the primary school. Bradley reported that he was not good at the class ICT activities because he couldn't enter the answers properly – the software was set up to reject wrong spelling – and he became frustrated entering the same answer over and over just to see it marked wrong every time, and when the computer made the sound for a wrong answer the rest of the class laughed at him. He liked the 'games' software because he wore a headset and only he could hear the sounds, although it would be OK if others could hear them too, since they were correct answer noises now! He did not like the AlphaSmart laptop because it did not have a mouse and the screen was too small so he could not look back to see what he was writing. His typing was very slow and it took him much longer to type than write by hand. He reported that now he had learned where everything was on the computer keyboard his typing was much faster, and he could see what he was writing on the bigger screen, he could even make the font bigger and change the colour of the screen – and that was good too.

By the time he transferred to secondary school, Bradley was a proficient laptop user and had added text-to-speech software and a portable scanner to his package. He was consistently placed in the top 2 per cent of his year group throughout the secondary years and, using his laptop for exams, easily achieved university entrance qualifications.

———————————

Bradley's primary school routinely issued AlphaSmart laptops to dyslexic students but did not offer students any keyboarding skills tuition. Discussion with primary staff revealed that neither his class teacher nor the learning assistant felt confident with computers and both lacked any experience of dyslexia support software. The successful introduction of ICT at secondary school to support Bradley's dyslexia was largely due to the evaluation of his individual needs, the intensive tuition he was given to develop keyboarding skills and frequent practice using the software.

As Bradley's experience demonstrates, it is important to match ICT provision to the specific needs of individuals and to provide training and practice in the use of both hardware and software in order to use them successfully (Crivelli in Peer and Reid 2001: 223). Equally important is the need for staff training in ICT so that they can offer effective support to their students.

Supporting developing literacy

There is an increasing range of software available designed to improve the basic reading skills of dyslexic students. These may take the form of flash cards, games or reading comprehension exercises – many similar to text-based reading programmes – but having the advantage that dyslexic students do not have to persist with reading interventions at which they have already experienced failure. Many dyslexic students need substantially greater practice in structured activities to help them achieve the literacy skills that other students master – apparently – effortlessly. There are many interesting and varied software programs available that provide dyslexic students with a more enjoyable learning environment and do not lead to the same level of fatigue as using printed text and notebooks. Many of these programs are designed to give frequent, positive feedback to the user, which generates improved self-esteem due to success (Peer and Reid 2003: 66–70).

Dyslexic learners do not feel threatened by the computer and find it an endlessly patient teacher. This is also true for bilingual dyslexic learners who are faced with not only acquiring speech and understanding of an additional language but also with acquiring literacy in the new language, so software packages that support mono-linguistic dyslexic learners will be of equal – or greater – help to them.

Laptop computers supporting access to the secondary curriculum

Laptop computers are, arguably, the most important support for dyslexic students in the secondary school – provided that students are taught to use software, are given time to practice with this and that subject teachers encourage laptop use.

Some subject teachers place obstacles in the way of laptop use, sometimes unintentionally destroying the school's support provision for dyslexic – and other – students. This is often the result of misunderstandings about computer use and lack of knowledge about dyslexia and how it may affect individuals' classroom performance. Some teachers are convinced that dyslexic students can write faster and more neatly if they put more effort into the task, and that giving them laptop computers encourages laziness – but the notion that improved handwriting 'will come' if enough practice is given is a false one, usually based on incomplete knowledge about how dyslexia affects individuals and the fine motor difficulties that make it impossible for students to write fluently and legibly. Some dyslexic students' handwriting may deteriorate after a laptop is introduced, possibly because of the physical differences between the multi-sensory nature of keyboarding and the upper body movements required for handwriting, but others will produce improved work (Thomson 2007e: 15).

Some people think that using laptop computers in class gives dyslexic students some sort of unfair advantage over others – ignoring the fact that their dyslexia places them at a disadvantage – so anything that helps them to approach the same level as their classmates cannot be considered unfair. Some students find the dyslexic's laptop use distracting at first, but they soon get used to it – if there are no games on the machine, they will lose interest quickly.

The subject teacher's role is to deliver the subject curriculum and monitor students' progress in this, so when dyslexic students access materials using computer software and their work is presented legibly using word processors, they should praise this and make sure the laptop is always available. However, some subject teachers, aware of the organisational difficulties of their dyslexic students, worry that they may lose their work, or even lose the whole laptop – as they do with note/text books – but if work is backed up on the school network, they can access this from any computer. Practical concerns about space and electrical outlets in the classroom and the possible need for technical support that might disrupt a lesson do need to be addressed and most schools are able to make provision that is only minimally intrusive. Arrangements can be made for printing to be done at a time and place that will minimise any disruption in class (Cogan and Flecker 2004: 79; and **Photocopiable 9.1** on p. 145).

Schools could develop a protocol for laptop use that sets out arrangements for the identification of those dyslexic students who would benefit from laptop use, and the procedures in place for matching students with appropriate equipment and training in its use. Although all students receive ICT tuition, dyslexic students may require more time and different software to support developing keyboarding skills. They will be permitted to use ICT in examinations if they normally use it in the classroom, so they need to practice as much as possible in order to gain confidence and skill prior to assessments (Cogan and Flecker 2004: 93–5).

Not all dyslexic students may be able to make effective use of laptop computers but many who have not been able to write easily may find their powers of expression unlocked with the use of specialised software packages. Such ICT use allows dyslexic students to keep up with their peers in subject classrooms and produce a standard of work that more closely reflects subject knowledge and ability than handwritten work does.

Speech recognition (SR)

Speech (or voice) recognition software may be particularly helpful for dyslexic students, especially those already familiar with computers and word processing. It is possible – with training and practice – to dictate, edit and format text directly into any application. Text-to-speech features provide immediate feedback. Not only does its use greatly improve dyslexic students' self-confidence, it also gives them a level of independence in their learning that they may have never before achieved. SR use also reduces the need for additional adult support to read, scribe and transcribe for dyslexic students.

Possible problems using SR software in school:

- SR requires a powerful, modern laptop with good quality speech input.

- SR software learns an individual voice so students cannot 'share' the laptop.

- Good dictation skills are needed – work should be planned in advance.

- A subject classroom may not be a good place to use SR because of background noise.

- Speech has to be clear and unaccented – without slang.

There is growing awareness in schools of the potential of SR to increase access to the curriculum for dyslexic students but approaches and success vary widely – some dyslexic students use SR routinely as their main means of writing and recording work, but others have found it difficult to implement with any success at all (Nisbet *et al.* 1999: 77–9).

ICT use in examinations

Use of word-processing packages by dyslexic candidates in examinations is now fairly common practice, but this does require considerable prior learning, especially the development of fast, accurate keyboarding skills and individuals trying out a range of software packages in order to find the combination that suits them. Schools must then negotiate the use of the chosen package with the examining body and ensure that agreed hardware and software are available to the individual for all assessments. A natural development from such arrangements is the introduction of on-line and accessible digital examination papers. These have already been introduced at some universities for some subjects, and the Scottish Qualifications Authority (Nisbet *et al.* 2006: 11) has been investigating and piloting possibilities for providing these in national examinations – exam papers come on CD and students can listen to text as well as read it. Answers can be entered directly into a paper or produced using a word-processing application; printing is done at the end of the exam.

ICT use clearly leads to increased independence for dyslexic students at secondary school, and supports improvements in reading, writing and search skills by using new materials and methods instead of text-based approaches that have already failed. However, the introduction of ICT requires considerable investment in resources – hardware (including laptop computers allocated to individuals), a wide range of software and time for the training of dyslexic learners in the use of these. Equally important is the need for the training of school staff in the use of ICT so that they can pass on expertise to dyslexic students.

Further reading

NISBET, P., SPOONER, R., ARTHUR, E. AND WHITTAKER, P. (1999) *Supportive Writing Technology*, Edinburgh: The University of Edinburgh, retrieved 23 July 2007 from http://callcentre.education.ed.ac.uk/About_CALL/Publications_CAA/Books_CAB/Supp_Writing_CAC/supp_writing_cac.html#download.

UNIVERSITY OF EDINBURGH with The CALL Centre (2006) *Symposium on Accessible Digital Curriculum Resources for Children and Young People with Additional Support Needs*, Edinburgh, 8 March 2006 from www.callcentrescotland.org.uk/digitalcurriculum/index.html.

Supporting and working with parents of dyslexic students

In this chapter, readers will:

- become aware of the legislation related to partnership with parents and voluntary organisations;

- consider the factors associated with dyslexia that might impact parent–school relationships;

- examine the relative roles of parents, the school, and the education authority when an investigation/assessment of dyslexia is proposed;

- explore the need to discuss support provision for individual dyslexic students with their parents;

- look at how parents could be involved in arrangements for and preparation of dyslexic students for tests and exams.

Many parents of dyslexic children discover their own dyslexia only when their children are diagnosed. It is very important that teachers realise that dyslexia runs in families and that they cannot expect support to be readily available at home.

Disability and Special Educational Needs legislation (see Table 4.1, p. 32) places certain rights and responsibilities on Local Authorities:

> A local education authority must arrange for the parent of any child in their area with special educational needs to be provided with advice and information about matters relating to those needs.
>
> (Section 332A, Education Act, DfEE 1996)

Partnership with parents

Legislation across the UK requires parents of children with special educational needs to be treated as partners by education authorities and this partnership will play a key role in promoting a culture of cooperation to enable dyslexic students to achieve their potential in the secondary curriculum (DfES 2001a: 16–19).

Parent Partnership Services (England and Wales) and similar provision in Scotland and Northern Ireland are set up by local authorities to provide parents with access to information, advice and guidance in relation to their children's dyslexia so they can make informed educational decisions (Reid 2004: 97–9). Information should be available in community languages and in alternative formats for those parents who are unable to access this through conventional means. Flexible services should be offered including arranging for a parent supporter or interpreter for meetings, and referral to voluntary dyslexia organisations or support groups that offer advice.

Many schools have fully developed policies and procedures that encourage parental involvement, but if parents' previous experience of the education system was not good they may be uncomfortable and anxious when meeting teachers. Schools should offer additional support and encouragement for parents, providing user-friendly information and procedures that:

- take account of parents' feelings and value their knowledge and experience of their children;

- enable parents to play an active role in their children's education;

- ensure that parents understand procedures and are fully informed;

- seek constructive ways of reconciling different viewpoints;

- recognise that parents themselves may have communication barriers;

- accept the need for flexibility in the timing and structure of meetings.

(Reid 2004: 97–101)

If a student's dyslexia is identified for the first time at the secondary school, parents should have access to information, advice and support during the assessment process and be involved in discussion about any support provision. They should be informed about any entitlement their child may have within the authority's SEN framework and their views taken into account. Parents should be fully informed about school-based support provision and the purpose of proposed interventions explained. Information about local parent partnership services and voluntary groups should be provided – but no referral to any support group should be made without permission.

The voluntary sector

Schools should also try to develop partnerships with local support groups or voluntary organisations, which have a unique and important contribution to make in providing a range of services and support for parents (Fawcett in Peer and Reid 2001: 268). The voluntary sector may provide schools with details of services that they offer to be passed on to parents. Some groups offer to attend consultations and meetings or contribute to training opportunities. Voluntary groups often take a proactive role in education perhaps participating in advisory groups and other consultative activities in order to promote and share their experiences of best practice.

Parent–school relationships

Many parents of dyslexic children will need a high level of support from the school, so communications should always be positive and constructive. When contacting parents, teachers should consider the additional difficulties and stress that they often experience – *guilt* about the possibly inherited nature of dyslexia, *frustration* due to feelings of helplessness, *anxiety* about the long-term implications of dyslexia and *exasperation/despair* because it is so hard to convince teachers that parents really do know their children well (Thomson 2007d: 8). Teachers' own possible confusion about the nature of dyslexia and concern about students' distress and frustration may unintentionally contribute to parents' anger at the school through something as simple as homework triggering behavioural problems at home and creating stress for the whole family. Parents need to be assured that agreed support is in place in all subject classes and that subject teachers are fully aware of their child's dyslexic profile.

The SENCo – or nominated member of senior staff – and specialist dyslexia teachers should be available to provide sympathetic contact for parents of dyslexic students. A school's dyslexia policy should be sent home, outlining likely support provision and a dialogue with parents begun to explore students' individual needs – essential for a shared understanding that there is no 'quick fix' or 'cure' for dyslexia and that supporting the progress of dyslexic students will be a long process, even with specialist teacher input (Houston 2002: 7).

The specialist dyslexia/support teacher should explain to parents the possible social and emotional impact of dyslexia on teenagers (Fawcett in Peer and Reid 2001: 270–1). Some dyslexic students perform well orally but experience difficulty with literacy or meet unexpected barriers to learning in the subject curriculum, and they may respond by developing behaviour problems – disruptive outbursts, refusal to cooperate in class, becoming moody and withdrawn – that parents and subject teachers may not relate to dyslexia.

A whole school approach to anticipating difficulties caused by the wider implications of dyslexia such as organisational and short-term memory problems might be agreed with parents to deal with problems such as:

- sending home notes and newsletters;

- relaying verbal messages;

- homework.

Measures taken to involve parents in dealing with known dyslexic issues, especially homework may de-fuse possible conflict and reduce the stress for all concerned.

Working with parents

Requesting a dyslexia assessment

Many parents assume that any difficulties that their children may experience are identified and dealt with at the primary school – but this is not always the case with dyslexia for a number of reasons:

- A student may have developed very good strategies for dealing with dyslexic problems in the classroom.

- A student may hide dyslexic difficulties by behaving badly, complaining of illness or truancy.

- Class teachers may not be fully aware of how dyslexia affects learning.

Many able children can achieve the standards required for national tests despite their dyslexia, and the fact that they are actually underachieving is not apparent, even to them. Sometimes it is not until students embark on the secondary subject curriculum that they meet unexpected barriers to learning, indicating dyslexia. For many secondary students, image is all-important and anything that makes them different from peers is rejected, resulting in dyslexic students deliberately underachieving and associating with slower learners or the disaffected to save themselves from being embarrassed by the effects of their dyslexia in a subject classroom (Hales in Peer and Reid 2001: 239).

Parents are usually first to observe changes in their children that suggest dyslexia, and they may request the school to investigate this. In order to make sure that such requests are dealt with in accordance with the legislation, the names of the person responsible for SEN and the specialist dyslexia teacher should be known to office staff and published in any school prospectus/handbook issued to parents. The procedures for requesting any SEN assessment are published by the education authority, and schools should ensure that this information is easily accessible to parents, and that all teachers know and follow the required procedures. Since the legislation places time limits on schools and authorities for carrying out assessments, parents would be well advised to follow up any verbal request in writing to start this process.

Some authorities arrange for dyslexia assessments to be carried out by (or in cooperation with) the educational psychology service and parents may have to give explicit permission for this and be made aware that involving an agency outside the school may delay or extend the process. Some schools offer investigation of possible dyslexia by their specialist teacher, and give parents the choice of whether to proceed with a full assessment once this is complete. Some parents are not satisfied with the arrangements for assessment provided by the school/authority, and others may disagree with the contents of the reports produced and take their children for independent assessment. This is permitted by the legislation and schools should be prepared to accept any report produced by a suitably qualified individual – they may request details of an assessor's training and qualifications, especially if application for access arrangements for exams is proposed.

If the school identifies the presence of dyslexia, and parents are contacted, some general information about dyslexia and its manifestations should be sent to them as well as any checklist or questionnaire for completion. It is important at this stage to offer parents an appointment with the school's dyslexia specialist to address any concerns.

Once a student's dyslexia has been investigated and a profile produced, additional information should be sent home including details of any proposed support provision – at this stage parents should be invited to meet with teachers to discuss the nature and purpose of the support. Parents should be assured that information about the dyslexic profile will be given to all of their child's subject teachers, along with suggested strategies for support in the classroom.

Support provision in the secondary curriculum

Those students' whose dyslexia is very severe or co-morbid with another condition probably already have individual educational plans describing additional support provision and parents will be involved in regular meetings to review and evaluate these. Pupils whose dyslexia was identified prior to transfer to secondary school may have learning plans that contain details of support and resources to be put in place to remove barriers to learning in the curriculum including any arrangements for individual literacy or numeracy tuition, and parents should be involved in any reviews of these. Those students whose dyslexia was not identified until secondary school, may have developed excellent coping strategies that disguise the extent of their dyslexic difficulties and parents may not at first see the need for any support to be provided, so any barriers to students' attainment should be identified and strategies for minimising these discussed.

It should be made clear to parents that placing extra adult support in subject classes is not always the most effective support for meeting dyslexic students' additional needs (Wearmouth in Peer and Reid 2001: 46). Sometimes parents obtain advice and information from the Internet – or from other parents – that describes support provision in general terms – or in different countries – and this may not be appropriate for their children at their school. Some may demand daily reading tuition or that a learning assistant is placed in all classes to support their child because dyslexic students elsewhere have this provision, even though this is not appropriate and is rejected by the student concerned. The individual nature of dyslexic difficulties should be made clear so that parents understand that although there are some support strategies that suit many dyslexic students, such as ICT use, every student has different needs that must be met in the way that suits the individual best, no matter what suits other dyslexic students.

Some schools and authorities have information packs that can be issued to all parents of dyslexic children, explaining their policies and the support that might be provided. It is important that such packs are individualised for parents so that they have a clear picture of how dyslexia affects their child in the curriculum and what support is appropriate in different circumstances. Many voluntary organisations provide downloadable parents guides (Dyslexia Scotland 2005b) and advice sheets on many topics, and those that are relevant to an individual student's profile could be printed and included in a personalised information package to be sent home.

An education authority must inform parents of their rights under Dispute Resolution legislation, but it is important that schools make every effort to reach agreement with parents about appropriate support for their dyslexic children without requiring recourse to this process.

Arrangements for tests and exams

Parents of dyslexic students should be informed when access/alternative arrangements are being considered for national tests and examinations (see **Photocopiable 10.1**, p. 146) – and schools should discourage them from using terms such as exam concessions or accommodations, as these are misleading and seem to imply that exams are somehow made easier for dyslexic candidates. It should be stressed that access arrangements are provided to make sure that dyslexic students can understand the test/exam paper in much the same way as the support provided in class allows them to follow the curriculum. All students sit the same exam paper and this is not changed for dyslexic students, though enlarged print or digital versions might be supplied. The exam is not made any easier and the variations in conditions – e.g. extra time allowances or computer use – make no difference to the way the exam paper is marked. Pupils are awarded the grade that matches their actual exam performance.

Students and their teachers select the arrangements they feel will meet their needs best in each examination, according to the demands of the subject and the style of assessment. Any access/alternative arrangements made for dyslexic students will reflect the support already in place in subject classes. Parents should also be informed about the extensive paperwork required by some examining bodies when application is made for access arrangements and alerted that additional assessment of a student's dyslexia may be required, including referral to educational psychology services. They should be kept informed of the outcome of applications for access/ alternative arrangements.

The differences between national testing and subject exams should be made clear to parents so that they understand the differences between tests to determine the actual level of performance reached and those that examine an individual's subject attainment.

Suggested reading

BRITISH DYSLEXIA ASSOCIATION (2008) *Getting Help for your Child* from the BDA website at www.bdadyslexia.org.uk/gethelp.html.

DYSLEXIA SCOTLAND (2005) *Dyslexia: A Brief Guide for Parents* from the DS website at www.dyslexiascotland.org.uk/.

OSTLER, C. (1999) *A Parent's Survival Guide*, Surrey: Ammonite Books.

REID, G. (2004) *Dyslexia: A Complete Guide for Parents*, London: John Wiley & Sons.

Glossary

Access (England, Wales and NI) Changes made to the context of an assessment in order to ensure that a dyslexic person can access an examination.

Access (Scotland) Level of certification of national qualifications – Access 1, 2, 3.

Additional support Provision that is additional to, or otherwise different from, the educational provision made generally for children and young people.

Alternative assessment arrangements (Scotland) Changes made to the context of an assessment in order to ensure that a dyslexic person can access an examination.

Assessment An ongoing process of gathering, structuring and making sense of information about a child or young person in order to inform decisions about actions necessary to maximise their potential.

Auditory discrimination Receptive activity including selection, identification and classification of perceived sounds.

Auditory-sequential memory Ability to receive, hold, recall and use auditory information in the sequence in which it has been presented.

Automaticity Development of the ability to perform certain actions without conscious thought.

Cognitive ability A measure of learning skills such as memory and phonological awareness.

Co-morbidity Disabilities occurring together – e.g. dyslexia and ADHD where there are both sets of symptoms, some common to both conditions.

Directionality Knowledge of a person's own sidedness, used to orient the body to the directions in space – e.g. something is 'in front' of you because it is your front.

Disability (Disability Discrimination Act 1995) – A physical or mental impairment that has a substantial and long-term adverse effect on a person's ability to carry out normal day-to-day activities.

Dispute resolution (Scotland) The involvement, under the Education (Scotland) Act 2004, of an independent adjudicator to review a disagreement between parents, or a young person, and an education authority.

Double deficit hypothesis A deficit in two essential skills that gives rise to the lowest level of reading performances, constituting the most severe form of dyslexia.

EAL English as an additional language.

Fine motor skills Skills requiring precision and accuracy, such as handwriting.

Fluency Ability of the brain to do or think something over and over and more and more quickly without being conscious of it. When applied to reading, means that the reading is smooth, with appropriate expression, intonation and use of punctuation to communicate meaning.

Gross motor skills Skills involving hand–eye coordination, e.g. catching a thrown object.

Individual Education Plan/Programme (IEP) A planning, teaching and reviewing tool. It is a working document for teachers recording key short-term targets and strategies for an individual pupil.

Learning assistant (Support for Learning assistant) A non-teacher providing in-school support for pupils with special/additional support needs and/or disabilities – one of a group within the broader classification of 'teaching assistant'.

Learning disability A condition that either prevents or significantly hinders somebody from learning basic skills or information at the same rate as most people of the same age.

Motor planning Ability to organise, plan and then execute new or unpractised motor tasks.

Multi-sensory learning Employing more than one learning style.

Multi-sensory teaching Using more than one teaching style to accommodate the differing learning preferences of pupils.

National Curriculum Inclusion Statement (England, Wales and NI) Detailed overarching statement on inclusion within the National Curriculum; states the principles schools must follow to ensure all pupils have the chance to succeed, whatever their individual needs and the potential barriers to learning, including modification of the National Curriculum.

Oppositional/Defiant Disorder (ODD) A recurrent pattern of negativistic, defiant, disobedient, and hostile behaviour toward authority figures that persists for at least six months – characterised by the frequent occurrence of: losing temper, arguing with adults, actively defying or refusing to comply with the requests or rules of adults, deliberately doing things that will annoy other people, blaming others for his or her own mistakes or misbehaviour, being easily annoyed by others, being angry and resentful, being spiteful or vindictive.

Personal Learning Plan (PLP) This helps children, young people and parents to be clear about the goals of learning, including those for personal development. Its focus is on supporting dialogue among teachers, parents, children and young people, and ultimately about engaging children and young people in their own learning. The purpose of record keeping and documentation is to support the process of personal learning planning.

Phonological Relating to language sounds.

Phonological deficit Inability to segment written words into underlying phonological components – impairs decoding, preventing word identification – a lower-order linguistic deficit blocking access to higher-order linguistic processes and to gaining meaning from text. The language processes involved in comprehension and meaning are intact, but cannot be used, as they can be accessed only after a word has been identified.

Psychometric tests Measure all aspects of mental ability, personality, intelligence, aptitude.

Readability Easily calculated measure of the degree of difficulty of text.

School Action (England, Wales and NI) Interventions additional to or different from those provided as part of the differentiated curriculum.

School Action Plus (England, Wales and NI) Advice or support from outside specialists, so that alternative interventions additional to or different from those strategies provided for the pupil through School Action can be put in place.

Screening Short investigative tests and measures such as observation/ interviews by a specialist to see if dyslexic traits are present.

SEN Special educational needs.

SEN coordinator (SENCo) (England, Wales and NI) Member of staff who has responsibility for coordinating SEN provision within a school.

Short-term (working) memory deficit Difficulty remembering what has just been said or read or following a sequence of classroom instructions that have just been issued.

Spatial awareness Knowledge of one's position in space relative to other objects – applies to concepts such as up/down and involves problems negotiating obstacles.

Specific learning difficulties (SpLD) Sometimes a synonym for dyslexia but these include separate conditions that overlap with dyslexia, e.g. dyspraxia, dysgraphia.

Spoonerism Transposing the first sounds in two words.

Standard score Test results recalculated for comparison with performance of a particular group.

Standardised tests Norm-referenced tests providing a measurement that is compared with the average scores of a standardised sample.

Underlying difficulties Underachievement is assumed to be due to poor academic skills and performance is equated to ability – the impact of dyslexia ignored.

Visual discrimination   Ability to see similarities and differences and to pick out details in visual information – may refer to objects, shapes, letters, words.

Visual memory   Ability to store images presented through visual stimuli.

Working memory   *See* **short-term memory.**

Glossary of exam language
(photocopiable)

Although most exam language is taught to you as part of your study of a subject, sometimes the wording of questions can be a little obscure. Below is a brief glossary of some exam terminology – add to this as appropriate for your subjects.

Analyse   Describe the main ideas, show how they are connected to each other and why they are important.

Assess   Find the weak points and the strong points of the subject in question.

Comment on   Say what *you* think about the subject.

Compare   Write about similarities and differences in the subjects.

Contrast   Show how two or more subjects are different from each other.

Criticise   Say what you think on a subject, giving your views for and against and back them up with facts and theories.

Define   Give the exact meaning of the word or phrase. Give an example, if you know one, and if you have memorised the definition, then write it down.

Describe   Give a full account of the word or phrase; give a picture in words; (*except in Maths* where it means draw, e.g. describe an arc).

Develop   Start with a given, often simple, idea and use your subject knowledge to expand it into something more complex.

Differentiate   Say clearly what the differences are.

From: Thomson, Moira (2008) *Supporting Students with Dyslexia in Secondary Schools*, London, Routledge © Moira Thomson 2008

Discuss   Describe the subject in detail and, if there are two sides to a question, give the points for and against.

Distinguish   This word is usually followed by 'between'; say clearly what makes the difference between the subjects.

Enumerate   List the main ideas by name and number.

Essential   (adjective) Most important aspects, what *must* be present.

Evaluate   Say what you think on the subject, giving the good and bad points, saying how valuable or useful the subject is.

Evidence   (noun) Give facts as proof to support your answer.

Examine   Write what you have to say *for* and *against* a subject, say which side you support and *give reasons* for your support.

Expand   Take a simple idea and add to it, showing how it might grow; *in Maths* usually requires a compact item to be opened out, e.g. expand an equation.

Explain   Give reasons (how/why) for something; say how something works.

Express   Often found in *Maths* exams; put in a different way, e.g. express as a fraction; in *other subjects*: say what is asked, e.g. express your opinion of.

Give   Pick some key factors and name them.

Hypothesis   (noun) An *informed guess* that can be changed or amended in the light of the evidence available (plural – hypotheses; verb – to hypothesise).

Identify   Say what something is; name the main point(s).

Illustrate   Use examples to make a point clear.

Interpret   Give the meaning in your own words using examples, where necessary, to make the meaning clear.

Justify   Say why you think that the answer is what it is and give reasons for why you feel that way.

List State the fact with no details.

Name Identify or make a list.

Option A choice.

Outline Write about the main ideas but do not go into detail.

Prove Show that the answer is true by giving the steps needed to reach it.

Relate Show how things connect; they may be similar or one may make another act in a certain way.

Review Give an overall view of the important facts of the subject and give your own views backed up by facts when necessary.

State Write the main points in a brief, clear way.

Suggest Often found in Geography exams; using all that you have learned, say what the answer *might* be; give a possible reason for something.

Summarise Bring together the main points and write about them in a brief, clear way.

Trace Tell the story of a subject in order, starting at the beginning and following it through to the end without going into detail.

From: Thomson, Moira (2008) *Supporting Students with Dyslexia in Secondary Schools*, London, Routledge © Moira Thomson 2008

Dyslexia assessment instruments

Electronic materials

Lucid Research www.lucid-research.com/

All tests come with instruction manuals and on-line support via the website.

1 Lucid Rapid Dyslexia Screening

Purpose of software: To help teachers to identify potential dyslexia in 15 minutes.

Features: Quick screening for dyslexia – short tests of:

- phonological processing ability
- working (auditory-sequential) memory
- phonic decoding skills.

2 Lucid Assessment System for Schools, LASS Secondary 11–15

Purpose of software: Diagnosis and assessment of dyslexia.

Features: Tests of:

Cognitive measures:

- visual memory
- auditory verbal memory
- phonic skills
- phonological skills.

Attainment measures:

- single-word reading
- sentence reading
- spelling
- non-verbal reasoning.

3 Lucid Research, LADS – Lucid Adult Dyslexia Screening

Purpose of software: Designed to *screen* for dyslexia at 16+.

Features: Four assessment modules, which measure:

- word recognition
- word construction
- working memory
- non-verbal reasoning.

4 LADS Plus – Lucid Adult Dyslexia Screening (Plus Version)

Purpose of software: Identification of dyslexia in wider populations that may include individuals who have non-standard educational backgrounds, low general ability, and/or poor English language skills, such as:

- young offenders
- persons who have had disadvantaged childhoods
- persons who have had disrupted or non-standard schooling
- ethnic minorities.

5 Lucid Ability – Verbal and Non-verbal Reasoning Suitable for Non-Readers

Purpose of software: Assessment of verbal and non-verbal skills – validated against conventional instruments including WISC-III and BAS II. Results are available immediately in three forms:

- standard scores
- centile scores
- age equivalents.

An overall measure of General Conceptual Ability (GCA) is provided.

6   *Lucid ViSS*

Purpose of software: Identification of visual stress causing reading problems – predicts those who should benefit from using coloured overlays or lenses.

Dedicated website www.visual-stress.com.

NFER Nelson http://shop.nfernelson.co.uk

7   *Turner, M. and Smith, P. (2004)* Dyslexia Screener, *London: NFER Nelson and SEMERC*

Purpose of software: To diagnose dyslexia through evaluation of:

- non-verbal reasoning
- phonics
- spelling
- visual search
- reading
- verbal reasoning.

8   *Sacre, L. and Masterson, J.* Single Word Spelling Test, *London: NFER Nelson (digital version 2007)*

Purpose of software: To assess spelling attainment of 6–14-year-olds.

Provides:

- spelling ages
- percentile ranks
- standard scores.

www.snapassessment.com/INFphon.htm

9   *Weedon, C. and Reid, G. (2003)* SNAP (Special Needs Assessment Profile), *Oxford: Hodder & Stoughton*

Purpose of software: diagnostic assessment and profiling of 5–14 age group. It breaks down Specific Learning Difficulties into 15 different areas.

Tests for identification and assessment of dyslexia

1   *Fawcett, A. and Nicolson, R. (2004)* Dyslexia Screening
Test – Secondary (DST-S), *Oxford: Harcourt Assessment*

Purpose of the test: To identify secondary school students at risk of dyslexia by:

- providing a profile of strengths and weaknesses

- identifying those who still experience difficulties

- providing data to support access/alternative arrangements requests in exams.

2   *Neale, Marie D. (1997)* Neale Analysis of Reading Ability
(2nd rev. British edn), *London: NFER Nelson*

Purpose of the test: To test oral reading of students from 6 to 13 and to diagnose their individual needs – provides measures of reading accuracy, comprehension and rate and detailed diagnostic information.

3   *Vincent, D. and De la Mare, M. (1985) (Consultant – Helen
Arnold)* The New Reading Analysis, *London: NFER Nelson*

Purpose of the test: To assess the accuracy and comprehension of reading – appropriate for students of an average reading ability in the 7–9+ age range and for older readers reading at the level of the average seven-year-old.

4   *Frederickson, N., Frith, U. and Reason, R. (1997)* Phonological
Assessment Battery, *London: NFER Nelson Standardised
Edition (PhAB) 6 years to 14 years 11 months*

Purpose of test: To assess the phonological skills required for reading.

5   *Guron, L.M. (2003)* Wordchains, *London: NFER Nelson*

Purpose of test: Early identification of word recognition difficulties.

6   *Sacre, L. and Masterson, J.* Single Word Spelling Test,
London: NFER Nelson

Purpose of test: To assess spelling attainment of 6–14-year-olds.

Identifies:

- spelling ages

- standard scores

- percentile ranks

- progress scores

- structured analysis of spelling errors

- supplementary assessments

- structured spelling lists.

7 Copyright-free Tests and Assessment Procedures for use by qualified individuals

Downloadable from the **Dyslexia Action** website www.dyslexiaaction.org. uk/Page.aspx?PageId=177.

- sentence completion test

- one-minute reading test

- digit memory test

- Perin's Spoonerism Task

- writing speed norms

- scaled scores and their equivalents

- Peabody Picture Vocabulary Scale-III: suggested Anglicisation

- revised adult dyslexia checklist

- non-word decoding test.

8 Checklists for identification and assessment of dyslexia

Downloadable from Dyslexia Scotland at www.supportingdyslexicpupils. org.uk/6.html.

- dyslexia – self-esteem issues

- dyslexia – skills inventory

- fine motor assessment (writing).

Photocopiable materials

PHOTOCOPIABLE 1.1

Dyslexia Indicators Checklist - Secondary

Subject teachers are not expected to be able to diagnose dyslexia in their students, but some general indications of possible dyslexia – in addition to reading problems - are listed below. If a student is observed to experience several of these regularly in the classroom, tick the relevant boxes and enter details of the student concerned.

Please forward this form to_____for further investigation.

Pupil Name: _____   Class: _____   Date: _____

- ❑ Quality of written work does not adequately reflect the known ability of the student in the subject; has difficulty with planning and writing essays

- ❑ Good orally but very little written work is produced – many incomplete assignments

- ❑ Disappointing performance in timed tests and other assessments – may not complete these in the time allowed

- ❑ Poor presentation of work – e.g. illegibility, mixed upper and lower case, unequal spacing, copying errors, misaligned columns (especially in Maths work)

- ❑ Poor organisational skills – student is unable to organise self or work efficiently; carries either all books or wrong ones; frequently forgets to hand in work

- ❑ Sequencing poor – student appears to jump from one theme to another, apparently for no reason

- ❑ Inability to memorise (especially in Maths and Modern Languages) even after repeated practice

- ❑ Inability to hold numbers in short-term memory while performing calculations

- ❑ Symbol and shape confusion (especially in Maths)

- ❑ Unable to carry out operations one day which were done adequately on a previous occasion

- ❑ Unable to take in and carry out more than one instruction at a time, or confuses a sequence of instructions, doing things in the wrong order

- ❑ Poor depth perception – e.g. clumsy and uncoordinated, difficulty judging distance, catching balls, etc.

From: Thomson, Moira (2007) *Supporting Dyslexic Pupils in the Secondary Curriculum*, Edinburgh, Dyslexia Scotland © Dyslexia Scotland and Moira Thomson 2007

❑ Poor self-image – lacking in confidence, fear of new situations – e.g. may often erase large quantities of written work

❑ Weaknesses are surprising because in other ways this student is bright and alert, demonstrating areas of strength and ability

❑ Tires quickly and work seems to be a disproportionate return for the effort involved in producing it; takes frequent rests/breaks when working

❑ Easily distracted – either hyperactive or daydreaming (circle which)

❑ Has a poor sense of direction and still confuses left and right

❑ May be often late for class for no apparent reason

❑ Other – please give details

Teacher: Subject:

Have concerns been mentioned to parents?   YES/NO

Have parents requested/agreed to further investigation?   YES/NO

If YES, give date of this request/agreement _____

Photocopiable materials

From: Thomson, Moira (2007) *Supporting Dyslexic Pupils in the Secondary Curriculum*, Edinburgh, Dyslexia Scotland © Dyslexia Scotland and Moira Thomson 2007

PHOTOCOPIABLE 2.1

Investigating Dyslexia – Observation Schedule

Pupil: **Date:**

Subject: **Time of day:**

> **Description of main lesson activity:** (circle) *Practical Reading/writing Teacher talk Copying*
> Notes on content, teaching strategies used, differentiation, resources etc.

Pupil's learning behaviour should be scanned at approximately 1 minute intervals and learning behaviour recorded under the following headings:

	ON TASK		OFF TASK
Reading		Talking	
Writing		Shouting out	
Listening		Noisy	
Talking		Doodling	
Watching		Fidgeting	
Copying		Dreaming	
Questioning		Distracted	
Answering		Disruptive	
Drawing		Out of seat	
Practical work		Interfering	
Waiting			
Other			

Comment on:
Settling down to work:

Following instructions: Written Spoken

Asking for help:

Nature of teacher interventions:

Co-operation with others:

Completion of set tasks:

PHOTOCOPIABLE 2.2

Investigating Dyslexia – Observation Schedule

Pupil: Date:

Subject: Time of day:

> **Description of main lesson activity:** (circle) *Practical Reading/writing Teacher talk Copying*
> Notes on content, teaching strategies used, differentiation, resources etc.

Pupil's learning behaviour should be scanned at approximately 1 minute intervals and learning behaviour recorded under the following headings:

Dyslexia Indicator	Frequency observed
poor auditory discrimination	
asks what was said (page number etc)	
can't remember spoken instructions	
appears not to hear teacher's talk	
poor visual discrimination	
complains can't see (e.g. the board)	
squints at text, moves book a lot	
difficulties copying	
asks others what text says	
difficulty organising work & desk	
appears not to try to start work	
does not write continuously	
writes very little	
often asks how to spell words	
avoidance strategies (e.g. ill, no pencil)	
tires quickly, takes rests/breaks	
does not volunteer answers	
refuses to read aloud	
gets angry when struggling with task	

Comment on:

> Settling down to work:
>
> Following instructions: Written   Spoken
>
> Asking for help:
>
> Nature of teacher interventions:
>
> Co-operation with others:
>
> Completion of set tasks:

PHOTOCOPIABLE 3.1

Example of a checklist of underachieving behaviour

Subject Dept: _____

Pupil details: _____

Learning characteristics

☐ Is orally good but written work is poor – gap between expected and actual performance – may be reluctant to write at length because s/he cannot write as fast as s/he thinks

☐ Is apparently bored, may appear to be absorbed in a private world

☐ Often abandons set work before finishing, having mastered content/process

☐ Can follow complex instructions easily, but may prefer to do things differently

☐ Works independently, but finds many reference sources superficial

☐ Good problem-finding skills, but reluctant to solve these once identified

☐ Inventive in response to open-ended questions, able to form but not test hypotheses

☐ At ease in dealing with abstract ideas

☐ Shows a vivid imagination with unusual ideas

☐ Is very observant, perhaps argumentative, able to ask provocative questions

Behavioural characteristics

☐ Has a poor concentration span but is creative and persevering when motivated

☐ May be emotionally unstable – feelings of inferiority but outwardly self-sufficient

☐ Often restless and inattentive, lacks task commitment

☐ Prefers to work alone, rarely cooperates in group work

☐ Shows originality and creativity but quickly gets bored with repetitive tasks

☐ Has a narrow range of interests and hobbies with extraordinarily knowledge of obscure facts

☐ Appears to have little in common with classmates, being tactless and impatient with slower minds

☐ Has a quirky, sometimes adult, sense of humour

From: Thomson, Moira (2006) *Supporting Gifted & Talented Pupils in the Secondary School*, London, Paul Chapman Publishing: p. 21

PHOTOCOPIABLE 3.2

Summary of strategies for dealing with dyslexia in the subject classroom

Reading for information
- Try to ensure that print is not the only source of important information
- Highlight key information
- Use teacher-led class lessons
- Use small-group discussion
- Use tutorial groups
- Use video, audio or ICT presentation
- Give specific pages and paragraph references
- Number the lines of text
- Give source references for questions
- Ensure source materials are clearly legible
- Enlarge print and increase line spacing

Reading aloud
- **Never** ask the pupil to read aloud – <u>but</u> accept as a volunteer
- **Key information** should be read aloud only by a teacher or competent reader

Using reading exercises for testing subject knowledge – alternatives
- Set practical tasks as tests
- Instigate teacher-pupil discussion
- Provide the opportunity for drawing up, or completing charts, or making illustrations

Writing tasks
- Never issue blank notebooks/paper
- Arrange transcription of written work
- Provide copies of diagrams, charts, and so on
- Provide a framework for extended writing
- Encourage writing for later transcription
- Allow alternatives to handwriting:
  - scribe
  - laptop computer
  - word processor
  - Dictaphone
  - voice recorder

Copying
- Provide printed notes in advance
- Make photocopies of notes
- Scan text into computer
- Identify a copying partner
- Ensure that copies are made as soon as possible after a lesson

Inappropriate behaviour
- Check whether learners are seeking clarification of printed instructions
- Discuss the nature of set tasks before embarking on individual work
- Check that instructions are fully understood
- Ask pupils to repeat instructions aloud
- Encourage all pupils to work together

Poor organising ability
- Do not give complex verbal instructions
- Give only one instruction at a time
- Be realistic in setting tasks
- Do not automatically set unfinished reading or writing as homework
- Provide the opportunity for practice or rehearsals of tasks
- Structure set tasks
- Encourage correct use of homework diary and involve parents

continued

Effects of fatigue
- Give short, well-defined tasks
- Keep task structure simple
- Set time limits for tasks
- Teach appropriate pacing
- Vary the types of tasks
- Change activities often
- Set clearly defined targets
- Create an opportunity for purposeful movement

Poor self-image
- Remain aware of pupils' dyslexia
- Give praise for work well done
- Encourage oral contributions
- Do not ask to read aloud or copy
- Mark on <u>content</u> not presentation of written work
- Create opportunities for alternatives to written responses/presentations

Discussion
- Provide a structure for discussion
- Encourage all pupils to suggest explanations/test hypotheses

Different learning styles
- Present information in a variety of modes – video, ICT, teacher talk, and so on
- Present information in a variety of formats – text, tables, diagrams, and so on
- Allow opportunities for active learning by – discussion, role play, research/investigation, and so on

Number
- Issue square/lined paper
- Allow the use of calculators for all number work
- Provide training in the use of calculators
- Make addition and multiplication grids, ready-reckoners available
- Use a variety of approaches (including computer games) to develop and reinforce number facts

Symbols and shapes
- Issue templates of shapes to emphasise their different properties
- Provide ample opportunity for revision and reinforcement

Practical tasks
- Provide roller/sticky rulers
- Provide left-handed scissors/tools/instruments where appropriate
- Provide transparent rulers/instruments for reading scales, and so on
- Enlarge graphs to make small details more accessible

Mathematical language and technical terms
- Teach mathematical/technical terms
- Introduce a subject word bank
- Explain technical terms
- Highlight everyday words that have specific technical meanings
- Provide support for reading and writing, e.g. read instructions aloud
- Check language of assignments as well as mathematical content

Adapted from Dodds and Thomson 1999

PHOTOCOPIABLE 6.1

Supporting dyslexia in the secondary classroom

SUGGESTIONS FOR SUBJECT TEACHERS

Lesson planning

Secondary subject teachers may anticipate the possible additional support needs of dyslexic (and other) pupils when planning lessons and preparing materials. Dyslexic pupils may experience:

- short term (working) memory difficulties
- problems with auditory and/or visual processing – how the messages received from the ears and eyes are transmitted in the brain
- weak organisational skills
- directional confusion
- poor physical coordination.

Lesson delivery

Consideration might be given to the method of lesson delivery, which should be multi-sensory whenever possible. Teachers could:

- Use coloured chalk/pens when writing on the blackboard/whiteboard; use a light colour background and dark text on an interactive whiteboard or material presented via a data projector.
- Use graphs, charts and illustrations to explain subject content where possible.
- Avoid asking for too much writing – allow the use of strip cartoons, flow charts, mind maps etc to record lesson content.
- Use practical aids when teaching, e.g. templates, table squares, calculators, and so on

Support strategies for dyslexic pupils

Time

Remember that dyslexic pupils will be slow to process lesson content – they first have to process the words used, then process the meaning of these and this takes more time:

- Build-in additional practice time for dyslexic pupils to develop new skills.
- Allow extra time for dyslexic pupils to organise thoughts and complete set work.
- Provide scaffolding and outline formats to guide the flow of work.
- Assume that dyslexic pupils need extra time for various activities so be flexible – find this time by adding extension work for other pupils.
- Remember that dyslexic pupils take much longer to complete homework than other pupils so do not set too much. Check that tasks are written down correctly and that dyslexic pupils understand what is required.

continued

PHOTOCOPIABLE 6.1 *(continued)*

Methodology

When actually delivering the lesson, subject teachers might incorporate additional support strategies:

- Avoiding asking dyslexic pupils to read aloud unless they volunteer to do so. This helps avoid humiliation and/or contributes to improving self-esteem.
- Arrange for text material to be read aloud – but first check that the level of material is appropriate. Audio/digital books could be very useful.
- Allow 'thinking time' to take account of dyslexic pupils' slower processing skills.
- Avoid giving answer before dyslexic pupils have had a chance to complete the work set – add 'extra' activities for other pupils to create this time.
- Allow dyslexic pupils to choose their preferred learning methods or tools, e.g. pictures, graphs, recording devices, computers, table squares, and so on
- Consider accepting answers in key words or in note form – this could help the dyslexic pupil write ideas down – but you may need to teach this skill.
- Limit the number of instructions given at one time and repeat a sequence of instructions throughout the lesson.

Individualising the curriculum

- Give individual attention when you can and encourage dyslexic pupils to ask for help when they need it.
- Seat dyslexic pupils near to you and encourage questions – perhaps arranging a signal indicating that help is required to avoid repeated pubic requests.
- Check that pupils understand any assignment/task set. It might be appropriate to issue a written note of this for more complex tasks.
- Present new information more than once and in various formats e.g. verbally, in diagrammatical format followed by demonstration/worked examples.
- Help dyslexic pupils to relate new concepts to past experience.
- Provide additional exercises to create the opportunity for over-learning.

Measuring progress

- When assessing progress, test orally at times, repeating questions as required and/or allow spoken responses or dictated answers.
- Try to include positive comments when marking work – these are rarely experienced by dyslexic pupils. Mark for content and not spelling/presentation.
- Measure individual progress rather than making comparisons with the rest of the class or specific attainment levels.

Working with parents

Try to maintain good communication with parents, perhaps use the homework diary for two-way communication. Keeping parents informed will enable frank discussion of any difficulties that arise and help gain their full cooperation to resolve problems quickly.

PHOTOCOPIABLE 8.1

Learning preferences

Traditionally, school subjects have been taught using an approach that relied on students learning by listening and writing. Those pupils whose natural learning style is not suited to this approach may not have learned effectively across the curriculum when they actually had not had the chance to learn in a way that suited them.

Understanding your preferred learning style can help you study more effectively by using techniques that improve the way you:

a) perceive information;

b) process information and;

c) organise and present information.

There are four generally accepted modalities of learning:

*   **Vi**sual

*   **A**uditory-verbal

*   **K**inaesthetic

*   **T**actile.

It is possible to identify these by simple observation of the features below:

*   **Visual** learners often look at the teacher's face intently, make lists, organise their thoughts, recall information by remembering how it was set out on a page.

*   **Auditory-verbal** learners prefer verbal instructions, solve problems by talking about them, use sound as memory aids, enjoy discussions.

*   **Kinaesthetic** learners learn best when they are involved or active, find it difficult to sit still for long periods and may use movement as a memory aid.

*   **Tactile** learners learn well in hands-on activities like projects and demonstrations and prefer to use writing and drawing as memory aids.

A simple way of finding your preferred learning style is to use **Photocopiable 8.2**. All you have to do is look at the activity listed in the column on the left, then decide which of the descriptions in the other three columns best describes your approach to each activity.

From: Thomson, Moira (2008) *Supporting Students with Dyslexia in Secondary Schools,* London, Routledge © Moira Thomson 2008

PHOTOCOPIABLE 8.2

Learning styles identification chart

This chart may help you find your learning style; read the left column and then choose the best answer from from the other columns. The column where most of your answers appear gives your preferred learning style (based on Colin Rose (1987) *Accelerated Learning*)

	Visual	Auditory	Kinesthetic and tactile
Reading	Do you like descriptive scenes and imagine the actions?	Do you enjoy dialogue and hear the characters talk?	Do you not like fiction and prefer true stories?
Spelling	Do you try to see the word?	Do you sound out the word or use a phonetic approach?	Do you write the word down to find if it feels right?
Talking	Do you use words such as see and imagine? Do you not talk much or like listening for long?	Do you use words such as hear and think? Do you enjoy listening but like to talk or interrupt?	Do you use words such as feel and touch? Do you use gestures and make faces?
Concentrating	Are you distracted by mess or movement?	Are you distracted by sounds or noise?	Are you distracted by activity going on around you?
Meeting someone you know	Do you forget names but remember faces or where you met?	Do you forget faces but remember names or what you talked about?	Do you remember best what you did together?
Try something new	Do you like to see demonstrations, diagrams or posters?	Do you prefer verbal instructions or talking about it with someone?	Do you prefer to get right down to try it?
Make or build something	Do you look at the instructions and the picture?	Ask someone for advice?	Do you ignore the instructions and work it out as you go?
Need help	Do you look for help pages or diagrams?	Do you ask someone for help, or talk yourself through it?	Do you keep trying to figure it out by trial and error?

From: Thomson, Moira (2006) *Supporting Gifted & Talented Pupils in the Secondary School*, London, Paul Chapman Publishing: p. 53

PHOTOCOPIABLE 8.3

Dyslexia and the school library

Libraries often present barriers to students with dyslexia who have difficulties in areas required for successful use of resources, which can be exacerbated by a library environment that fails to take account of the different needs of dyslexic students.

Potential barriers for dyslexic students to library use:

- They may avoid the library because of a history of literacy problems.
- Anxiety about access to text materials may result in them being unaware that the school library holds non-text resources.
- A catalogue that relies on alphabetical order and/or sequences of numbers and letters that have no obvious link to the location or content of the materials.
- Complex directional instructions for locating materials.
- Difficulties in determining from a 'blurb' or index if materials will actually be relevant to the task at hand.
- Embarrassment about approaching library staff/helpers and disclosing their dyslexic problems.

Suggested strategies to reduce barriers:

- Information leaflets and posters should use pictorial/diagrammatic information where possible, in an easily readable font on coloured paper - which could be matched to colours used to delineate subject areas, and so on.
- The layout of the school library needs to be considered carefully – perhaps using colour to delineate subject areas and different media types, and displaying floor diagrams to help with location.
- Extended loan periods should be available as dyslexic students require longer to locate and extract information from text. Extensive photocopying might be offered in collaboration with the specialist support team and subject departments when the demand on library resources is likely to be heavy – e.g. when a specific topic is set for a whole year group and extended loans are not possible. (Permitted under licence from the Copyright Licensing Agency or by the VIP amendment to the 1980 Copyright Act.)
- An 'ordering and fetching' service would allow materials to be delivered to students, or a teaching assistant or student helper could go with a dyslexic student to help locate materials. Any such services should be clearly advertised to subject and support staff as well as students and any 'booking' requirements easy to access.
- Audio books should be available where possible. This requires liaison with, e.g. the English Department about set texts – well in advance of every session so that the librarian has time to order audio versions – or to arrange for recordings to be made in school (for nominated students under to VIP amendment to the Copyright Act).
- Technological support should be available – e.g. a scanner to scan text for computer generated voice output; writing software for speech output, word prediction and spell check facilities; mind-mapping software.

Books on dyslexia should be available for subject teachers and dyslexic students in the school library.

From: Thomson, Moira (2008) *Supporting Students with Dyslexia in Secondary Schools,*
London, Routledge © Moira Thomson 2008

PHOTOCOPIABLE 8.4

Active revision

1 **Preparation** – Look at the material to be studied. Make sure it is legible.

- If it is not easy to read, type it into a computer using a spellchecker.
- If the text is clearly legible, scan it into a computer so you can alter the layout and/or use a screen reader.
- Arrange for the text to be recorded – you may need someone to read it aloud – then you can listen while studying the text.

You now have the choice of studying the text in the format you prefer – print, audio or on the computer.

2 **First study session** – Using your preferred version of the text, scan the whole piece to get an overview of the content. If you prefer an audio recording, use this together with a print version of the text.

- Think about the information you need to obtain from the text. Make a list of this and note any additional questions that occur to you.
- Read the whole text again. This time locate and highlight key words and key sentences/ideas. (NB – a key sentence is usually at the beginning of a paragraph.) When you identify a key idea, stop and read more closely, then make notes.
- Think about whether you now have enough information to answer your questions. Decide whether your notes have enough detail to answer these.

3 **Later study sessions** – Look at your list of questions and try to recall the information you found previously.

- If you have difficulty with finding or remembering enough to answer the questions, you may have to follow the whole procedure again.
- Don't worry if you have to repeat the first steps several times before you can recall enough information to answer your questions – everybody does!
- As more information is transferred into your long-term memory, it will become easier to remember facts and details.

4 **Structuring answers** – Once you are sure you can locate enough information to answer your questions, – practice doing this.
- Exam questions often use formal language and require structured answers (see Glossary of exam language, pp. 121–4).
- Producing these answers is a skill you can learn and improve in - a bit like practicing a piece of music or a sport. Draft answers and consider whether you are actually answering the question.
- Your skills get better with practise and the more you practise, the better you become – this works for answering exam questions too. Work on structuring your answers until you can respond to any type of question.

5 **Pacing study sessions** – Several short study periods spread out over a number of weeks will give you a better chance to keep information in your long-term memory than trying to cram it all in the night before an exam.

Laptop use by dyslexic students in the secondary classroom

A practical guide for subject teachers

Be prepared
- Make sure that laptop users sit near power points to avoid dead batteries.
- Beware of trailing cables – issue safety rules.
- Check that students' desks are big enough – laptop use may need two desks together.
- Make sure the rest of the class know that no-one else may use the laptop.
- Arrange printing details in advance.
- If possible, insist the laptop is set up before the start of the lesson to avoid distractions.
- Make sure the student has a subject template already saved with name and subject already there.
- Ensure each day's work is labelled and saved at the start of the lesson and updated regularly.
- If the lesson involves drawing diagrams, plan the method in advance with the student – e.g. do by hand and scan; draw onto the screen, and so on.
- If the lesson requires tables to be completed, make sure there is a template available.
- If the student has screen reading software, keep a spare headset available.
- Insist that all sound effects are turned off when no headset is used.
- Arrange how homework will reach you – e.g. e-mail; saved on school network in prearranged file; printed and handed in, and so on.

Decide:
- When a lesson will not be suitable for a laptop and tell the student in advance.
- How you want work to be set out – give the student an instruction sheet at first.
- How you want completed work stored – electronically or hard copy.

Encourage the student:
- To use the laptop for all writing and reading if a text reader is used.
- To sit correctly – both feet on the floor, back straight, two hands on the keyboard, and so on.
- To take proper care of the laptop and have a routine for dealing with it as hardware.
- To elaborate on text later – adding various features not part of the standard layout.
- To organise all work in properly labelled folders.

Beware of:
- Games – ask parents to remove these.
- The possibility of students 'sharing' work, especially for homework – develop rules.
- Students' love of strange fonts, bold text and odd colour combinations – have rules for these.
- Greater concentration on the laptop than on the lesson content.
- Other students' resentment of laptop use – point out it is the equivalent of wearing glasses and arrange for, e.g. whole class sessions in a computer lab.
- 'Technical' excuses for incomplete or 'lost' work.

Accept that:
- The novelty will soon wear off and other students will get used to the laptop use.
- Laptop screens will be seen by other students – so walk behind the user often to discourage inappropriate displays.

From: Thomson, Moira (2008) *Supporting Students with Dyslexia in Secondary Schools*, London, Routledge © Moira Thomson 2008

PHOTOCOPIABLE 10.1

Information for parents

Access/alternative arrangements for examinations

The range of alternative arrangements available to dyslexic learners in exams from primary school to higher education is very wide, and should reflect the support or strategies normally used by the student in the classroom. Some support may not be easily identifiable by students or even the teacher – e.g. when teachers routinely read materials to the whole class, they may not identify this as use of a reader by a dyslexic student.

Dyslexic candidates should be given a combination of access/alternative arrangements for formal exams that allow them to demonstrate attained standards with the least possible level of aid. There should be no assumption that a dyslexic candidate will need the same arrangement for every assessment. For example, a dyslexic candidate may need a reader and extra time for an exam with long reading passages, but not for one where the reading content is much less.

The range of access/alternative arrangements that may be available for assessments includes:

- Linguistic support
  - ▶ a reader
  - ▶ a scribe
  - ▶ digital exam papers
  - ▶ transcription – with correction – of the written paper.
- Extra time allowances
- Use of ICT
  - ▶ word processors
  - ▶ use of spellchecker
  - ▶ software that reads text/digital question papers
  - ▶ software that supports writing, e.g. predictive lexicon
  - ▶ voice recognition software.
- Use of other technological aids
  - ▶ calculator use in non-calculator Maths papers
  - ▶ use of spelling aids.
- Transcription without correction to remove illegibility
- Rest periods/supervised breaks where extra time makes a paper very long
- Adapted question papers
  - ▶ papers printed on different coloured paper
  - ▶ enlarged print papers
  - ▶ digital question papers (on computer).

The actual arrangement applied to a test or exam in a subject will usually match the support provided in class or at home for normal course work. However, a dyslexic learner may be able to cope with the reading demands of a subject when additional time is given, a reader is needed in a timed exam because the amount of extra time required to process the text is more than the examining body allows, or would make the exam paper so long that fatigue becomes a limiting factor.

Some arrangements may not be permitted in some subjects or for certain types of examination – the school holds information about this, which is updated annually.

Arrangements for National Curriculum tests and Standardised tests may differ from those described above – always check with the school.

From: Thomson, Moira (2007) *Supporting Dyslexic Pupils in the Secondary Curriculum*, Edinburgh, Dyslexia Scotland © Dyslexia Scotland and Moira Thomson 2007

References

ANGUS COUNCIL EDUCATION DEPARTMENT (2006) *Support for Learners Policy*, pp. 153–4, retrieved 23 June 2007 from www.angus.gov.uk/atoz/pdfs/sflpolicy.pdf.

ASSOCIATED BOARD OF THE ROYAL SCHOOLS OF MUSIC (2005) *Guidelines for Candidates with Dyslexia or Other Learning Difficulties*, retrieved 20 July 2007 from www.abrsm.org/resources/specialNeedsDyslexiaOther LearningDifficulties.pdf.

BACKHOUSE, G., DOLMAN, E. AND READ, C. (edited by Greenwald) (2007) *Dyslexia: Assessing the Need for Access Arrangements during Examinations: a Practical Guide* (3rd edn), Evesham, Worcs: PATOSS & JCQ.

BRITISH DYSLEXIA ASSOCIATION (2006a) *Indications of Dyslexia*, retrieved 3 March 2007 from www.bdadyslexia.org.uk/indications.html.

—— (2006b) *Dyslexia Style Guide*, retrieved 10 March 2007 from www.bdadyslexia.org.uk/extra352.

—— (2006c) *Modern Foreign Languages and Dyslexia*, retrieved 20 June 2007 from www.bdadyslexia.org.uk/mfl.html.

—— (2007) *What is Dyslexia?*, retrieved 2 May 2007 from www.bda dyslexia.org.uk.

—— (2008) *Getting Help for your Child* from the BDA website at www.bdadyslexia.org.uk/gethelp.html.

BRITISH PSYCHOLOGICAL SOCIETY (1999) *Dyslexia Literacy and Psychological Assessment*, Leicester British Psychological Society, pp. 16–17, 44, 64, 122.

CALDER, I. (2004) 'Including pupils with dyslexia: how can classroom assistants help?', Paper presented at BDA Conference, University of Warwick, March 2004, retrieved 14 March 2007 from www.bdainternationalconference.org/2004/presentations/mon_s6_b_5.shtml.

CLINE, T. AND SHAMSI, T. (2000) *Language Needs or Special Needs? A Literature Review*, London: DfES Publications, p. 15, retrieved 10 July 2007 from www.dfes.gov.uk/research/data/uploadfiles/RR184.doc.

COGAN, J. AND FLECKER, M. (2004) *Dyslexia in Secondary School: A Practical Handbook for Teachers, Parents and Students*, London: Whurr, pp. 2–3, 25–8, 71, 79, 93–5, 117, 132–4, 149, 180–1, 288.

CRIVELLI, V., THOMSON, M. AND ANDERSSEN, B. (2004) 'Using ICT to support dyslexia learners at secondary school', in G. Reid and A. Fawcett (eds) *Dyslexia in Context: Research, Policy and Practice*, London: Whurr.

CROMBIE, M. AND MCCOLL, H. (2001) 'Dyslexia and the teaching of modern foreign languages', in L. Peer and G. Reid (eds) *Dyslexia: Successful Inclusion in the Secondary School*, London: David Fulton.

———— AND SCHNEIDER, E. (2004) *Dyslexia and Modern Foreign Languages: Gaining Success in an Inclusive Context*, London: David Fulton.

DARGIE, R. (2005) *Dyslexia and History*, London: David Fulton.

DEPARTMENT FOR EDUCATION AND EMPLOYMENT (DFEE) (1996) Education Act, retrieved 2 June 2008 from www.opsi.gov.uk/acts/acts1996/ukpga_19960056_en_1.

DEPARTMENT FOR EDUCATION AND SKILLS (DFES) (2001a) *SEN Code of Practice*, London: DfES, pp. 16–19, 57, 65, 67, 68–9, 68–72, 71–2, 74–5, 75–6, 77, retrieved 26 February 2007 from www.teachernet.gov.uk/_doc/3724/SENCodeOfPractice.pdf.

———— (2001b) *SEN Toolkit*, pp. 21, 27–8, retrieved 16 March 2007 from www.teachernet.gov.uk/wholeschool/sen/sentoolkit/.

———— (2001c) *Guidance to Support Pupils with Dyslexia and Dyscalculia*, pp. 2, 9, retrieved 21 May 2007 from http://publications.teachernet.gov.uk/eOrderingDownload/DfES-0512-2001.pdf.

———— (2004) *Removing Barriers to Achievement*, pp. 56–8, 60, retrieved 23 May 2007 from www.everychildmatters.gov.uk/ete/sen/.

———— (2006) *Secondary National Strategy*, retrieved 20 July 2007 from www.standards.dfes.gov.uk/secondary/.

———— /BRITISH DYSLEXIA ASSOCIATION (2005) *Achieving Dyslexia Friendly Schools Information Pack*, p. 29, retrieved May 2007 from www.bdadyslexia.org.uk/dfs.html.

DEPARTMENT OF EDUCATION NORTHERN IRELAND (1996) *Code of Practice on the Identification and Assessment of Special Educational Needs*, pp. 14–24, 22–4, 71–3, retrieved 20 June 2007 from www.deni.gov.uk/the_code_of_practice.pdf

———— (2002) *Report of the Task Group on Dyslexia*, p. 59, retrieved 29 May 2007 from www.deni.gov.uk/dyslexia.pdf.

DISABILITY RIGHTS COMMISSION (2002a) *Disability Discrimination Act 1995: Part 4: Code of Practice for Schools*, pp. 34, 40, 44, retrieved 23 June 2007 from www.drc-gb.org/thelaw/practice.asp.

———— (2002b) *Guide for Schools*, p. 10, retrieved 23 June 2007 from www.drc.org.uk/library/publications/education/a_guide_for_schools_england.aspx.

DODDS, D. AND THOMSON, M. (1999) *Dyslexia: An In-service Training Pack and Handbook for Teachers*, Edinburgh: City of Edinburgh Council, Education Department.

DYSLEXIA ACTION (2005) *What is Dyslexia?*, retrieved 12 July 2007 from www.dyslexiaaction.org.uk/Page.aspx?PageId=26.

DYSLEXIA SCOTLAND (2005a) *Teachers' Guide*, p. 5, retrieved 12 June 2007 from www.dyslexiascotland.org.uk/documents/Guide%20for%20Teachers%20A4.pdf.

—— (2005b) *Dyslexia: A Brief Guide for Parents*, retrieved 11 July 2007 from www.dyslexiascotland.org.uk/documents/Guide%20for%20Parents%20A4.pdf.

—— (2006) *Dyslexia: Suggestions for Teachers*, www.dyslexiascotland.org.uk/documents/Dyslexia%20%20Suggestions%20for%20Teachers.pdf.

DYSPRAXIA FOUNDATION (2007) *Dyspraxia in Children*, retrieved 11 June 2007 from www.dyspraxiafoundation.org.uk/services/gu_introduction.php.

EADON, H. (2004) *Dyslexia and Drama*, London: David Fulton.

ELLIOT, D.L., DAVIDSON, J.K. AND LEWIN, J. (2007) *SCRE Research Report No 125: Literature Review of Current Approaches to the Provision of Education for Children with Dyslexia*, commissioned by HM Inspectorate of Education, The SCRE Centre, University of Glasgow, retrieved from www.scre.ac.uk/resreport/rr125/index.html.

FAWCETT, A. (ed.) (2001) *Dyslexia: Theory and Good Practice*, London: Whurr Publishers, pp. 39–44, 130–1, 141, 287.

GALABURDA, A.M., MENARD, M.T. AND ROSEN, G.D. (1994) 'Evidence for aberrant auditory anatomy in developmental dyslexia', *Proceedings of the National Academy of Sciences*, USA, Vol. 91, August, pp. 8010–13, Medical Sciences, retrieved 6 May 2007 from www.pnas.org/cgi/reprint/91/17/8010.

——, LOTURCO, J., RAMUS, F., FITCH, R.H. AND ROSEN, G.D. (2006) 'From genes to behavior in developmental dyslexia', *Nature Neuroscience*, Vol. 9, pp. 1213–17 published online 26 September 2006, retrieved 6 May 2007 from www.nature.com/neuro/journal/v9/n10/abs/nn1772.

GIVEN, G.K. AND REID, G. (1999) *Learning Styles: A Guide for Teachers and Parents*, St Annes-on-Sea: Red Rose Publications, pp. 15–16, 56, 81–3.

GRAY, R. (2001) 'Drama: the experience of learning', in L. Peer and G. Reid (eds) *Dyslexia: Successful Inclusion in the Secondary School*, London: David Fulton.

GRIFFITHS, M. (2002) *Study Skills and Dyslexia in the Secondary School: A Practical Approach*, London: David Fulton.

HENDERSON, A. (1998) *Maths for the Dyslexic: A Practical Guide*, London: David Fulton.

——, CAME, P. AND BROUGH, M. (2003) *Working with Dyscalculia*, Marlborough, Wilts.: Learning Works, pp. 124, 127.

HOLMES, P. (2001) 'Dyslexia and Physics', in L. Peer and G. Reid (eds) *Dyslexia – Successful Inclusion in the Secondary School*, London: David Fulton.

HONEY, P. AND MUMFORD, A. (1986) *The Manual of Learning Styles*, Maidenhead: Peter Honey Publications.

HOUSTON, M. (2002) *Dyslexia: An In-service Training Pack and Handbook for Primary Teachers*, Edinburgh: City of Edinburgh Council, pp. 4, 25, 28.

HOWLETT, C.A. (2001) 'Dyslexia and Biology', in L. Peer and G. Reid (eds) *Dyslexia – Successful Inclusion in the Secondary School*, London: David Fulton.

IRLEN, H. (1991) *Reading by the Colors*, New York: Perigee (2001), pp. 29–51, 72, 176–8.

JOINT COUNCIL FOR QUALIFICATIONS (JCQ) (2007–8) *Access Arrangements and Special Consideration Regulations and Guidance Relating to Candidates who are Eligible for Adjustments in Examinations 2007–8*, pp. 5, 4–28, 9–12, 12, 13–14, 19, 20, 21–2, 32, 34–6–7, 37–8, 65, 62–82, 80, 81, retrieved 20 February 2008 from www.jcq.org.uk/attachments/published/428/Final%20%ORAG%2007-08.pdf.

JORDAN, I. (2000) *Visual Dyslexia: A Guide for Parents and Teachers*, Barnetby-Le-Wold: Desktop Publications, pp. 20–2.

KAY, J. AND YEO, D. (2003) *Dyslexia and Maths*, London: David Fulton, pp. 14–15.

KELLY, D. AND GRAY, C. (2000) *Educational Psychology Services (England): Current Role, Good Practice and Future Directions*, DfES, pp. 4–6, 84, retrieved 10 July 2007 fromwww.teachernet.gov.uk/_doc/7378/EPWG%20Research%20Report.pdf.

LUCID RESEARCH (2003) *Fact Sheet 21*, LASS Junior and LASS Secondary case studies, retrieved 17 July 2007 www.lucid-research.com/documents/factsheets/FS21_LASScasestudies.pdf.

—— (2003) *Fact Sheet 24: How Accurate is My Screening Device?*, retrieved 23 July 2007 from www.lucid-research.com/documents/factsheets/FS24v02_HowAccurateScreeningDevice.pdf.

—— (2007) *Fact Sheet 4: Lucid's Product Research and Evaluation Studies*, retrieved 23 July 2007 from www.lucid-research.com/documents/factsheets/FS04_ResearchAndEvaluationStudies.pdf.

MCKAY, N. (2004) 'The Case for Dyslexia Friendly Schools' in Reid, G. and Fawcett, A. (eds) *Dyslexia in Context: Research, Policy and Practice*, London: Whurr.

—— (2005) *Removing Dyslexia as a Barrier to Achievement*, Wakefield: SEN Marketing, pp. 5, 15, 46, 52–9, 114–18, 140–1, 144–9, 157, 198–202, 203–5, 214.

MELLERS, C. (2000) *Identifying and Supporting the Dyslexic Child*, Desktop Publications www.ic-online.co.uk/em/Detail/it080003.htm.

MILES, T.R. AND MILES, E. (1999) *Dyslexia: A Hundred Years On* (2nd edn), Berkshire: Open University Press.

―― AND WESTCOMBE, J. (eds) (2001) *Music and Dyslexia: Opening New Doors*, London: Whurr.

MILTON KEYNES COUNCIL (2003) *Dyslexia Policy*, Milton Keynes Council Education Department, retrieved 20 June 2007 from www.milton-keynes. gov.uk/schools/documents/M30736__Milton_Keynes_Dyslexia_Policy.pdf.

MONTGOMERY, D. (ed.) (2003) *Gifted and Talented Children with Special Educational Needs: Double Exceptionality*, London: NACE/Fulton Publications, pp. 7–9, 8.

THE NATIONAL ASSEMBLY FOR WALES (2006) *Inclusion and Pupil Support*, pp. 19, 41–4, 61, retrieved 28 June 2007 from www.wales.gov.uk/inclusion andpupilsupport.

NATIONAL INSTITUTE OF MENTAL HEALTH (2006) *Attention Deficit Hyperactivity Disorder*, retrieved 10 July 2007 from www.nimh.nih.gov/ publicat/adhd.cfm.

NATIONAL UNION OF TEACHERS (2007) cited by Richard Garner in *The Independent*, 10 January, retrieved 8 June 2007 from http://education. independent.co.uk/news/article2140269.ece.

NISBET, P. AND AITKEN, S. (2007) *Books for All: Accessible Curriculum Materials for Pupils with Additional Support Needs*, Edinburgh: The University of Edinburgh, p. 3.

NISBET, P., SPOONER, R., ARTHUR, E. AND WHITTAKER, P. (1999) *Supportive Writing Technology*, Edinburgh: The University of Edinburgh, pp. 14, 77–9, retrieved 23 July 2007 from http://callcentre.education.ed.ac.uk/About_ CALL/Publications_CAA/Books_CAB/Supp_Writing_CAC/supp_writing_ cac.html#download.

―― , SHEARER, N., BALFOUR, F. AND AITKEN, S. (2006) *SQA Adapted Examination Papers in Digital Format Feasibility Study 2005–2006*, Edinburgh: University of Edinburgh, retrieved 10 June 2007 from http:// callcentre.education.ed.ac.uk/downloads/SQA/SQA%202006%20Evaluation %20Report%20Final%20anon.pdf.

NORTH AYRSHIRE COUNCIL (2007) *Dyslexia – An Information Leaflet*, Ayrshire: Educational & Psychological Services North Ayrshire Council, p. 12.

NORTHAMPTONSHIRE COUNTY COUNCIL (2006) *Guidelines: Specific Learning Difficulties: Dyslexia*, pp. 3, 6, 7, retrieved 18 June 2007 from www.northantsdyslexia.co.uk/Northants_Dyslexia_Guidelines%5B1%5D.pdf.

OFSTED (1999) *Pupils with Specific Learning Difficulties in Mainstream Schools*, London: Ofsted, p. 6, retrieved 28 July 2007 from www.ofsted.gov. uk/assets/1129.pdf.

OGLETHORPE, S. (2002) *Instrumental Music for Dyslexics: A Teaching Handbook*, London: Whurr.

OLIVER, J. (1999) *The Naked Chef*, London: Michael Joseph.

OSTLER, C. (1999) *A Parent's Survival Guide*, Surrey: Ammonite Books.

—— (2000) *Study Skills: A Pupil's Survival Guide*, Godalming: Ammonite Books, pp. 3, 35.

—— AND WARD, F. (2001) *Advanced Study Skills*, Wakefield: SEN Marketing, pp. 33–4, 45.

OTT, P. (1997) *How to Detect and Manage Dyslexia: A Reference and Resource Manual*, Oxford: Heinemann Educational.

PEER, L. (2001) *Dyslexia and its Manifestations in the Secondary School*, Presentation at the BDA International Conference, York 2001, retrieved 11 May 2007 from www.bdainternationalconference.org/2001/presentations/wed_s3_d_5.htm.

—— (2005) *Glue Ear: An Essential Guide for Teachers, Parents and Health Professionals*, London: David Fulton.

—— AND REID, G. (eds) (2000) *Multilingualism, Literacy and Dyslexia: A Challenge for Educators*, London: David Fulton, pp. 5, 59.

—— AND —— (eds) (2001) *Dyslexia: Successful Inclusion in the Secondary School*, London: David Fulton, pp. 3–6, 5, 10–11, 46, 54–6, 74–5, 92, 151, 217–18, 219, 232–3, 237, 239, 240, 268, 270–1.

—— AND —— (2003) *Introduction to Dyslexia*, London: BDA/Fulton, pp. 9–12, 10–11, 24–6, 27, 40, 41, 60–2, 68–70.

PORTWOOD, M. (2003) *Dyslexia and Physical Education*, London: David Fulton, pp. 81, 99.

PUGHE, J. AND TURNER, E. (2004) *Dyslexia and English*, London: David Fulton.

QUALIFICATIONS AND CURRICULUM AUTHORITY (QCA) (2007a) *The Secondary Curriculum Review*, retrieved 29 June 2007 from www.qca.org.uk/secondarycurriculumreview/.

—— (2007b) *Code of Practice*, pp. 41, 65, retrieved 21 July 2007 from www.qca.org.uk/libraryAssets/media/qca-07-3082_Unified_Code_Practice_web_April07.

—— /DFEE (1999) *The National Curriculum Inclusion Statement*, retrieved 29 May 2007 from www.nc.uk.net/nc_resources/html/inclusion.shtml.

REDGRAVE, S. AND BUZAN, T. (2001) *Head Strong: How to Get Physically and Mentally Fit*, London: HarperCollins.

REID, G. (2002) *Biological and Cognitive Dimensions Current Scientific Thinking*, retrieved 12 May 2007 www.lbctnz.co.nz/sld/dyslexia/current-thinking.html.

—— (2004) *Dyslexia: A Complete Guide for Parents*, Chichester: John Wiley & Sons, pp. 5–8, 14–15, 17, 57–9, 61–2, 63–6, 97–101, 110, 94–111.

—— AND FAWCETT, A. (eds) (2004) *Dyslexia in Context: Research, Policy and Practice*, London: Whurr, pp. 3–20, 224, 231–3, 253, 312.

—— AND GREEN, S. (2007) *100 Ideas for Supporting Pupils with Dyslexia*, London: Continuum International, pp. 4, 14–15, 56–7, 60, 65–6, 68, 94, 97.

——, DEPONIO, P. AND DAVIDSON PETCH, L. (2005) 'Identification, assessment and intervention: implications of an audit on dyslexia policy and practice in Scotland', *Dyslexia*, 11(3): 203–16. Available from www3. interscience.wiley.com/cgi-bin/abstract/110573341/ABSTRACT.

RENALDI, F. (2003) *Dyslexia and Design & Technology*, London: David Fulton and the BDA.

SCHNEIDER, E. AND CROMBIE, M. (2003) *Dyslexia and Foreign Language Learning*, Abingdon: David Fulton, pp. 4–5, 6–7.

SCOTTISH EXECUTIVE EDUCATION DEPARTMENT (2005) *Supporting Children's Learning Code of Practice*, Edinburgh: SEED, pp. 26–7, 36, 41–2, retrieved 30 November 2005 from www.scotland.gov.uk/Publications/2005/08/15105817/58187.

SCOTTISH QUALIFICATIONS AUTHORITY (2004) *Guidance on Assessment Arrangements for Candidates with Disabilities and/or Additional Support Needs*, pp. 1–3, 5, 6, 9, 10, 11–12, 15, 19–24, 27, 36, retrieved 18 July 2007 from www.sqa.org.uk/files_ccc/Alt_Assessment_Arrangements_final.pdf.

SHAYWITZ, S. (2003) *Overcoming Dyslexia*, New York: Vintage Books, pp. 52–4.

—— (2007) *The Brain and Dyslexia*, video interview with David Bolton, retrieved 8 May 2007 from www.childrenofthecode.org/interviews/shaywitz.htm#WhatBrainScans.

SKEATH, J. (2007) *Instrumental Teaching with the Dyslexic Pupil in Mind*, PATOSS Information Sheet 2, retrieved 3 July 2007 from www.patoss-dyslexia.org/Publications10.html.

SNOWLING, M.J. (2000) *Dyslexia* (2nd edn), Oxford: Blackwell, p. 138.

STOCKPORT METROPOLITAN BOROUGH COUNCIL (2006) *Guidance for Schools on the Disability Duty*, Andrew Webb corporate director of the Stockport Children & Young People's Directorate, SMBC, pp. 6, 27.

THOMSON, M. (2004) *Alternative Assessment Arrangements for Dyslexic Students*, Presentation at Dyslexia Scotland Conference, Edinburgh 2004, retrieved 22 July 2006 from www.thedyslexiashop.co.uk/pdfdocuments/MoiraThomsonAtDyslexiaScotland-20040911.

—— (2006) *Supporting Gifted & Talented Pupils in the Secondary School*, London: Paul Chapman Publishing, pp. 9, 17, 21, 29, 30, 53.

—— (2007a) *Supporting Dyslexic Pupils in the Secondary Curriculum. 1.1 Identification and Assessment of Dyslexia at the Secondary School*, Edinburgh: Dyslexia Scotland, pp. 5, 8, 9, 10.

—— (2007b) *Supporting Dyslexic Pupils in the Secondary Curriculum. 1.3 Classroom Management of Dyslexia at Secondary School*, Edinburgh: Dyslexia Scotland, pp. 8, 10, 13.

—— (2007c) *Supporting Dyslexic Pupils in the Secondary Curriculum. 1.4 Information for the Secondary Support for Learning Team*, Edinburgh: Dyslexia Scotland, p. 8.

—— (2007d) *Supporting Dyslexic Pupils in the Secondary Curriculum. 1.5 Supporting Parents of Secondary School Pupils with Dyslexia*, Edinburgh: Dyslexia Scotland, p. 8.

—— (2007e) *Supporting Dyslexic Pupils in the Secondary Curriculum. 1.6 Using ICT to Support Dyslexic Pupils in the Secondary Curriculum*, Edinburgh: Dyslexia Scotland, p. 15.

—— (2007f) *Supporting Dyslexic Pupils in the Secondary Curriculum. 1.7 Dyslexia and Examinations*, Edinburgh: Dyslexia Scotland, p. 14.

TURNER, E. AND PUGHE, J. (2003) *Dyslexia and English*, London: David Fulton, pp. 7–10, 64–5.

UNITED NATIONS EDUCATION, SCIENTIFIC AND CULTURAL ORGANISATION (UNESCO) (1994) *The Salamanca Statement*, retrieved 28 June 2007 from www.unesco.org/education/pdf/SALAMA_E.PDF.

UNIVERSITY OF EDINBURGH (2006) *Symposium on Accessible Digital Curriculum Resources for Children and Young People with Additional Support Needs*, Edinburgh, 8 March 2006, retrieved 30 July 2007 from www.callcentrescotland.org.uk/digitalcurriculum/index.html.

—— (2007) *Dyslexia at Transition* [DVDRom], Edinburgh: University of Edinburgh/SITC website at www.dyslexiatransition.org/.

—— with The CALL Centre (2007) *Accessible Digital Exams* retrieved 10 July 2007 from www.callcentresscotland.org/digitalexams/.

UNIVERSITY OF HULL (2007) *Dyslexia Case Studies*, Department of Modern Languages University of Hull, retrieved 20 July 2007 from www.hull.ac.uk/languages/about_us/support/dyslexia/guidline_dyslexia/case_study/index.html.

WEST, T.G. (1997) *In the Mind's Eye*, Amherst, NY: Prometheus Books.

WILLIAMS, F. AND LEWIS, J. (2001) 'Dyslexia and Geography', in L. Peer and G. Reid (eds) *Dyslexia: Successful Inclusion in the Secondary School*, London: David Fulton.

References

Index

Locators in *italics* indicate photocopiable materials.